The Apocryphal Gospels

TOOLS AND TRANSLATIONS

The Westar Tools and Translations series provides critical tools and fresh new translations for research on canonical and non-canonical texts that survive from the earliest periods of the Christian tradition to the Middle Ages. These writings are crucial for determining the complex history of Christian origins. The translations are known as the Scholars Version. Each work, whether a translation or research aid, is accompanied by textual notes, translation notes, cross references, and an index. An extensive introduction also sets out the challenge a text or research aid addresses.

EARLY CHRISTIAN APOCRYPHA

Editorial Board:
TONY BURKE
BRENT LANDAU
JANET SPITTLER

Translations of non-canonical texts out of the Christian tradition are offered as part of the Westar Tools and Translations series in cooperation with the North American Society for the Study of Christian Apocrypha (NASSCAL). The Early Christian Apocrypha series features fresh new translations of major apocryphal texts that survive from the early period of the Christian church. These non-canonical writings are crucial for determining the complex history of Christian origins. The series continues the work of Julian V. Hills, who edited the first six volumes of the series for Polebridge Press. *Studies in Christian Apocrypha* is a subseries to *Early Christian Apocrypha*. The subseries features studies (including short introductions, monographs, and thematic collections of essays) on Christian Apocrypha from any time period and in any of its myriad forms—from early "lost gospel" papyri, through medieval hagiography and sermons incorporating apocryphal traditions, up to modern apocryphal "forgeries."

Volume 1: *The Acts of Andrew*
Volume 2: *The Epistle of the Apostles*
Volume 3: *The Acts of Thomas*
Volume 4: *The Acts of Peter*
Volume 5: *Didache*
Volume 6: *The Acts of John*
Volume 7: *The Protevangelium of James*
Volume 8: *The Gospel of Pseudo-Matthew and the Nativity of Mary*
Volume 9: *The Apocryphal Gospels: Jesus Traditions outside the Bible*

The Apocryphal Gospels

Jesus Traditions outside the Bible

Jens Schröter

Translated by Wayne Coppins

CASCADE Books • Eugene, Oregon

THE APOCRYPHAL GOSPELS
Jesus Traditions outside the Bible

Early Christian Apocrypha 9
Westar Tools and Translation

Copyright © 2021 Jens Schröter. All rights reserved. Except for brief quotations in critical publications or reviews, no part of this book may be reproduced in any manner without prior written permission from the publisher. Write: Permissions, Wipf and Stock Publishers, 199 W. 8th Ave., Suite 3, Eugene, OR 97401.

Cascade Books
An Imprint of Wipf and Stock Publishers
199 W. 8th Ave., Suite 3
Eugene, OR 97401

www.wipfandstock.com

PAPERBACK ISBN: 978-1-6667-0670-3
HARDCOVER ISBN: 978-1-6667-0671-0
EBOOK ISBN: 978-1-6667-0672-7

Cataloguing-in-Publication data:

Names: Schröter, Jens, author. | Coppins, Wayne, translator.

Title: The apocryphal gospels : Jesus traditions outside the Bible / Jens Schröter; translated by Wayne Coppins.

Description: Eugene, OR : Cascade Books, 2021. | Westar Tools and Translations. | Early Christian Apocrypha 9. | Studies in Christian Apocrypha | Includes bibliographical references and index.

Identifiers: ISBN: 978-1-6667-0670-3 (paperback). | ISBN: 978-1-6667-0671-0 (hardcover). | ISBN: 978-1-6667-0672-7 (ebook).

Subjects: LSCH: Apocryphal Gospels—Criticism, interpretation, etc. | Apocryphal books (New Testament)—Criticism, interpretation, etc. | Apocryphal infancy Gospels.

Classification: BS2851 S37 2021 (print). | BS2851 (ebook).

Scripture quotations marked (NRSV) are taken from the New Revised Standard Version Bible, copyright © 1989 National Council of the Churches of Christ in the United States of America. Used by permission. All rights reserved worldwide.

To my friends and colleagues at the Research Centre
"Beyond Canon,"
University of Regensburg

Contents

Preface to the English Edition | ix
Abbreviations | xi

1 Introduction: Gospels in Early Christianity | 1
2 "Infancy Gospels": Narratives about the Birth and Childhood of Jesus | 14
3 Traditions about the Ministry of Jesus | 34
4 Traditions about the Suffering and Death of Jesus | 56
5 The Teaching of the Risen and Living Jesus | 75
6 Other Gospels | 99
7 Conclusion: The Significance of the Apocryphal Gospels for the History of Christianity | 106

Subject Index | 111
Author Index | 113

Preface to the English Edition

THE PRESENT WORK IS the revised and expanded English translation of my book *Die apokryphen Evangelien: Jesusüberlieferungen außerhalb der Bibel* (Munich: Beck, 2019). The work on the translation was completed in 2020–2021 during a fellowship at the Center for Advanced Studies "Beyond Canon: Heterotopias of Religious Authority in Ancient Christianity" at the University of Regensburg, funded by the German Research Foundation. I am grateful to my colleagues and friends for a wonderful time in Regensburg.

The book provides a survey of texts outside the New Testament that contain traditions about Jesus' birth, ministry, suffering, and death, as well as his appearances as the Risen One. Many of these texts are preserved only in fragmentary form. Quite a few of them were also unknown for a long time because they were lost in the sands of the Egyptian desert or left neglected on the shelves of museums and libraries. Since the end of the nineteenth century, many of them have been rediscovered, published, and translated into modern languages. In this way, our knowledge of the apocryphal Jesus traditions has been significantly expanded and changed.

Jesus traditions outside of the New Testament have played an important role in texts and visual presentations in the history of Christianity from early on. In particular, narratives about the birth and childhood of Jesus as well as traditions about his passion have deeply influenced Christian piety. Through the discovery of additional texts since the nineteenth century, the spectrum has expanded, for example, through writings that present the teaching of the risen Jesus and set entirely new emphases vis-à-vis the presentations of his activity in the Gospels of the New Testament.

In recent scholarship it has been asked whether the apocryphal gospels contain information that changes our picture of the historical Jesus.

PREFACE TO THE ENGLISH EDITION

This question will also be taken up in this book. The value of the apocryphal gospels—as can already be said at this point—resides not so much in their contribution to the historical reconstruction of Jesus' life, but in the fact that they provide glimpses of aspects of his ministry and passion that became meaningful in certain periods of the history of Christianity. Thus, the search for historically reliable traditions in the apocryphal gospels is less productive than the interpretation of these texts as receptions of the Jesus figure—his ministry, suffering and death, as well as his resurrection—in different periods of Christianity. This shall be sketched out in more detail by means of brief introductions to the relevant writings.

Many thanks are due to Wayne Coppins who has translated the book into English with admirable expertise, which has already proven itself on many occasions. As with previous projects, the collaboration with him was very enjoyable and productive. Likewise, I am thankful to the series editors, Janet Spittler, Tony Burke, and Brent Landau, for including the book in their series. Janet and Tony have read the manuscript very carefully and made many important and valuable comments that helped to improve it, both in language and content. I owe them a lot of thanks! Finally, I would like to thank the publisher, Cascade Books, an imprint of Wipf and Stock Publishers, for their friendly and competent collaboration.

Note: Translations from apocryphal gospels are from Bart D. Ehrman and Zlatko Pleše, *The Apocryphal Gospels*, unless otherwise noted.

Abbreviations

Ancient

Clement of Alexandria
    Exc.   *Excerpts from Theodotus*
    Strom.   *Miscellanies*

Didymus the Blind
    Comm. Eccl.   *Commentarii in Ecclesiasten*
    Comm. Ps.   *Commentarii in Palmos*

Epiphanius
    Pan.   *Panarion*

Eusebius of Caesarea
    Hist. eccl.   *Ecclesiastical History*

Hippolytus
    Haer.   *Refutation of all Heresies*

Irenaeus
    Haer.   *Against Heresies*

Jerome
    Comm. Ezech.   *Commentariorum in Ezechielem libri XVI*
    Comm. Is.   *Commentariorum in Isaiam libri XVI*
    Comm. Matt.   *Commentariorum in Matthaeum libri IV*
    Pelag.   *Adversus Pelagianos dialogi III*
    Vir. ill.   *De viris illustribus*

Justin Martyr
    1 Apol.   *First Apology*

ABBREVIATIONS

Origen

    Cel.   *Contra Celsum*
    Comm. Matt.   *Commentarium in evangelium Matthaei*
    Hom. Luc.   *Homiliae in Lucam*

Tertullian

    Scorp.   *Scorpiace*

Modern

BETL	Bibliotheca Ephemeridum Theologicarum Lovaniensium
CCSA	Corpus Christianorum: Series Apocryphorum
GCS	Die griechischen christlichen Schriftsteller der ersten [drei] Jahrhunderte
HTR	*Harvard Theological Review*
JBL	*Journal of Biblical Literature*
JSNTSup	Journal for the Study of the New Testament Supplement Series
LNTS	Library of New Testament Studies
NHMS	Nag Hammadi and Manichaean Studies
NHS	Nag Hammadi Studies
NTS	*New Testament Studies*
SBLSymS	Society of Biblical Literature Symposium Series
SNTSMS	Society for New Testament Studies Monograph Series
TENTS	Texts and Editions for New Testament Study
TU	Texte und Untersuchungen
WUNT	Wissenschaftliche Untersuchungen zum Neuen Testament
ZAC	*Zeitschrift für Antike Christentum*
ZKT	*Zeitschrift für katholische Theologie*

1

Introduction

Gospels in Early Christianity

"Apocryphal" Gospels and the Gospels of the New Testament

IN ADDITION TO THE Gospels of the New Testament, numerous other writings were composed about Jesus and persons in his immediate environment from an early time. These are often designated as "apocryphal"—i.e., hidden—gospels (the Greek word *apókryphos* means "hidden"). They contain numerous traditions about Jesus that go beyond the New Testament and sometimes even contradict it. If these writings are included, then the Jesus picture of Christianity becomes much more varied than the picture that can be derived from the Bible. Moreover, with regard to the designation "apocryphal," we have to ask in what sense these texts and their pictures of Jesus were or are indeed "hidden." Today, the apocryphal writings are readily accessible in critical editions and translations and are kept hidden by no one. They do not, however, belong to the Bible. How did there come to be a distinction between biblical and "apocryphal" gospels?

Around 180 CE, Irenaeus of Lyon composed a large-scale work in five books titled *Against Heresies*. In this writing he provides extensive critical engagement with teachings that, in his view, falsify the truth of the Christian confession. In Book 3, he comes to speak of the witness of the Gospels. Right at the beginning, he emphasizes that the gospel of God has been handed down to the church through Matthew, Mark, Luke, and John. This one gospel is, therefore, "four-formed," just as there are also four corners of the earth, four directions of the wind, and four cherubim before the throne of God (cf. Ezek 1:5–10 and Rev 4:6–11). The church spread over the whole earth is thus based on four pillars—namely, the four Gospels—and corresponds in this way to the order of the world, which reflects at the same time the Son of God's economy of salvation, as well as the four covenants that God made with Adam, Noah, Moses, and, finally, through the gospel.

There is obviously a problem concealed behind this forceful rationale of the *fourfold* form of the *one* gospel. Irenaeus is here defending this four-form against its contestation by people who claim that the Gospels are not free of error and that they also do not agree with one another. He also argues that Christian groups or individual teachers such as the Ebionites, Marcion, and the Valentinians rely on only one of the four Gospels and interpret it against its sense. According to him, this meaning discloses itself only from the overall consideration of the one four-formed gospel. Finally, Irenaeus writes about the followers of Valentinus, a Christian teacher who was active in Rome around 140 CE, and vehemently contests their claim that they possess more gospels than the four. In this context, he mentions a work that they call the "Gospel of Truth," although, in his view, it does not, in fact, contain the truth handed down by the apostles (on this, see the section on the *Gospel of Truth* in chap. 6).

Irenaeus' remarks show that it was by no means uncontroversial whether *all four* Gospels and *only these gospels* present the authoritative witness to Jesus. Irenaeus, therefore, defends the four-ness of the Gospels both against its reduction to only *one* gospel and against the view that there are, beyond them, other gospels that are to be regarded as authoritative. After all, it is by no means obvious that there should be precisely *four* gospels that contain the authoritative witness to Jesus for the church rather than one or two or three. One could just as easily supply rationales for these numbers—for example, with reference to the one God, to the two natures of Jesus Christ, or to the unity of the Father, Son, and Holy Spirit. The fact that Irenaeus insists that the truth is based on four Gospels can only be explained, therefore, by the circumstance that these four Gospels were already widespread and recognized in Christian communities. And this is also the only plausible explanation for why all three of the Gospels that are quite similar to one another—namely, the Gospels according to Matthew, Mark, and Luke (which are also called Synoptic, i.e., Gospels that can be read together)—made it into the New Testament and not just one or two of them. This is especially noteworthy in the case of the Gospel of Mark, whose content is almost completely contained in the Gospels of Matthew and Luke.

Irenaeus uses the term *euangelion*—the Greek word for "good news"—in two ways: 1) for the one gospel of Jesus Christ in its fourfold form, and 2) as a designation for the individual writings, which are called the "Gospel according to Matthew," the "Gospel according to Mark," the "Gospel according to Luke," and the "Gospel according to John." He presupposes, therefore, that the term *euangelion* is used as a designation for certain writings, while also being familiar with the meaning "good news (of Jesus Christ)." This double usage can be traced back to the beginnings of Christianity. In his letters, Paul frequently mentions "the gospel," which he describes more specifically as "the gospel of God," "the gospel of Jesus Christ," and, also, as "my gospel." With "gospel" Paul thus designates the message of God's saving action through Jesus Christ that he proclaims. In the Gospel of Mark, the term *euangelion* is then applied to the story of the ministry and fate of Jesus. The first sentence already reads "The beginning of the *euangelion* of Jesus Christ, the Son of God." *Euangelion* then occurs at multiple points in the Gospel of Mark: Jesus proclaims "the *euangelion* of God" (1:14), Jesus and the *euangelion* are mentioned alongside each other (8:35; 10:29); and the *euangelion* is to be proclaimed to all the nations in the world (13:10; 14:9). In the Gospel of Mark, the proclamation of the gospel of the imminent reign of God through Jesus is thus closely connected with his activity and fate.

From this starting point, the term *euangelion* became established as a designation for the narratives of the activity and fate of Jesus around the turn from the first to the second century. In order to distinguish them from each other, they were called "According to Matthew," "According to Mark," etc. These designations thus became necessary only in the moment at which multiple gospels were known and used together. The distinctive designation "Gospel according to + name" expresses the view that there is *one* gospel available in different forms. Later gospels—for example, the "Gospel according to Thomas" or the "Gospel according to Mary"—take up this designation and apply it to their presentations of Jesus. In this way, they claim that they likewise—or in contrast to the other gospels—contain authoritative Jesus traditions. By contrast, the plural "gospels" is first encountered around the middle of the second century CE in the writings of the Christian philosopher and martyr Justin. He designates the writings of the apostles as "memoirs" (memorabilia, a literary characterization that was also used for Xenophon's work *Memorabilia of Socrates*) and explains that the "Memoirs of the Apostles" are also called "gospels" (*1 Apol.* 66.2). Later, the term "gospel" was also used for writings that do not call themselves "gospel" and that sometimes differ clearly from the Gospels of the New Testament. In this expanded meaning it is applied to texts that present the origin, teaching, activity, and fate of Jesus in different literary forms. This expansion has led to the fact that in the orbit of the Gospels we also find texts that deal with persons from the environment of Jesus, such as his parents, John the Baptist, and Pilate. Writings that relate to the person of Jesus with biographical intent can be gathered together in this expanded understanding as "gospels and related literature."

The remarks of other early Christian theologians can be placed alongside those of Irenaeus. In his work *Stromateis* ("Patchworks" or "Miscellanies"), Clement of Alexandria, a contemporary of Irenaeus, quotes from a "Gospel according to the Egyptians," but notes that the quotation does not come "from one of the four Gospels handed down to us":

> This is why Cassian says, "When Salome inquired when the things she had asked about would become known, the Lord replied: 'When you (pl.) trample on the garment of shame and when the two become one and the male with the female is neither male nor female.'" The first thing to note, then, is that we do not find this saying in the four Gospels handed down to us, but in the Gospel according to the Egyptians. (Clement of Alexandria, *Strom.* 3.92.2–93.1, trans. Ehrman/Pleše; see also below on the *Gospel according to the Egyptians*)

In another place he quotes a saying from the *Gospel according to the Hebrews*:

> Which also is written in the Gospel according to the Hebrews: He who marveled shall reign, and he who reigned shall rest. (*Strom.* 2.45.5; see also 5.96.3; a similar saying occurs in the *Gospel of Thomas*, saying 2).

A letter of the bishop Serapion to one of his communities is quoted in Eusebius' *Ecclesiastical History*, which emerged in the first decades of the fourth century. The letter, which goes back to around 180 CE, mentions a "gospel under the name of Peter":

INTRODUCTION

> We, my brothers, receive Peter and all the apostles as we receive Christ, but the writings falsely attributed to them we are experienced enough to reject, knowing that nothing of the sort has been handed down to us.
>
> When I visited you, I assumed that you all clung to the true Faith; so without going through the "gospel" alleged by them to be Peter's, I said: "If this is the only thing that apparently puts childish notions into your heads, read it by all means." But as, from information received, I now know that their mind had been ensnared by some heresy, I will make every effort to visit you again; so expect me in the near future.
>
> It was obvious to me what kind of heresy Marcian upheld, though he contradicted himself through not knowing what he was talking about, as you will gather from this letter. But others have studied this same "gospel," viz. the successors of those who originated it, known to us as Docetists and from whose teaching the ideas are mostly derived. With their comments in mind, I have been able to go through the book and draw the conclusion that while most of it accorded with the authentic teaching of the Savior, some passages were spurious additions. These I am appending to my letter. (Eusebius, *Hist. eccl.* 6.12.3–6; trans. Williamson)

Finally, Origen, in his homilies on Luke, which he composed around 233/234 CE in Caesarea, notes that the church knows four Gospels, whereas the "heresy" knows many. Origen also lists some of the gospels of the "heresy": a gospel "According to the Egyptians," one that is called "According to the Twelve Apostles," another issued under the name of Basilides as well as gospels called "According to Thomas" and "According to Matthias":

> You should know that not only four Gospels, but very many were composed. The Gospels we have were chosen from among these gospels and passed on to the churches. We can know this from Luke's own prologue, which begins this way: "Because many have tried to compose an account." The words "have tried" imply an accusation against those who rushed into writing gospels without the grace of the Holy Spirit. Matthew, Mark, John, and Luke did not "try" to write; they wrote their Gospels when they were filled with the Holy Spirit. Hence, "Many have tried to compose an account of the events that are clearly known among us."
>
> The Church has four Gospels. Heretics have very many. One of them is entitled "According to the Egyptians," another

> "According to the Twelve Apostles." Basilides, too, dared to write a gospel and give it his own name. "Many have tried" to write, but only four Gospels have been approved. Our doctrines about the Person of our Lord and Savior should be drawn from these approved Gospels. I know one gospel called "According to Thomas," and another "According to Matthias." We have read many others, too, lest we appear ignorant of anything, because of those people who think they know something if they have examined these gospels. But in all these questions we approve of nothing but what the Church approves of, namely only four canonical Gospels. (*Hom. Luc.* 1.1–2; trans. Lienhard)

Thus, around the turn from the second to the third century, there were a multiplicity of writings that called themselves "gospel." Early Christian theologians, such as Irenaeus, Clement, and Origen, regarded the four Gospels according to Matthew, Mark, Luke, and John as the Gospels that contained the authoritative witness to Jesus of Nazareth, to his earthly activity, his resurrection, and his post-Easter appearances. Other writings that likewise claimed to be "gospels" were rejected by them as "heretical," "forged," or "apocryphal"—or at the very least, they were distinguished from the four Gospels. Other early Christian teachers—such as, e.g., Valentinus—by contrast, held a different view. According to their position, gospels that were composed later, either by themselves or their followers, or that besides the four Gospels of Mark, Matthew, Luke, and John circulated among early communities, were important testimonies for the meaning of Jesus and his message as well.

The fundamental commonality of the Gospels that were included in the New Testament lies in the fact that they tell the story of Jesus of Nazareth from its beginning to his death and resurrection. At the same time, there are numerous differences among them. These pertain, for example, to the chronological and geographical presentation of the activity of Jesus, the characterization of his person, and the individual characteristics of his activity, such as his teaching and his powerful deeds. These differences surface most clearly between the Synoptic Gospels, on the one hand, and the Gospel of John, on the other. The Synoptic Gospels recount the establishment of the reign of God through the activity of Jesus and especially through his healings, his table fellowship, and his teaching in parables. The Gospel of John, by contrast, presents Jesus as the incarnate divine "Word" through which God's glory has appeared in the world. This glory could be directly recognized in Jesus during his earthly activity:

INTRODUCTION

"The Word became flesh and we saw his glory" (John 1:14). In the Gospel of John, Jesus speaks in large discourses about himself as revealer of the truth of God, as "light of the world," "bread of life," and "good shepherd," and his deeds of power are "signs" of his divine origin. Thus, in comparison to the Synoptic Gospels, the Gospel of John more clearly views Jesus' earthly activity from the perspective of his resurrection and exaltation. It is already further removed from the historical events, even though it has also preserved historical information about the activity of Jesus.

Thus, the New Testament contains no unified picture of Jesus but different narratives with their own distinctive features. Historical-critical Jesus scholarship, which has its beginnings in the eighteenth century, therefore, saw itself confronted with the question of how a historical picture of the activity of Jesus can be produced from the Gospels' different pictures of Jesus. Here, it reached the view—which is largely accepted up to the present—that the Synoptic Gospels are closer to the historical reality of the activity of Jesus than the Gospel of John. Historical-critical presentations of Jesus, therefore, usually take their orientation from the Synoptic Gospels, whereas the Gospel of John is regarded as a theologically-oriented interpretation of the person of Jesus that arose later and that, in terms of its language and content, primarily reflects the theology of its authors or the circle from which it comes.

The New Testament Gospels probably originated between 70 and 100 CE. The Gospel of Mark, as the oldest of them, was composed around 70 CE and used by the authors of the Gospels of Matthew and Luke. The Gospel of John presupposes the other Gospels and interprets the activity of Jesus from a deepening theological perspective. In the second half of the second century CE, other gospels came into view. Some of these contain narratives about the birth and childhood of Jesus, others about his passion, and still others about his appearances and his teaching as the Risen One. These works usually presuppose the older Gospels and present the activity, teaching, and fate of Jesus in their own distinctive ways. In addition to the Gospels of the New Testament, they make recourse to other traditions, for example, to sayings of Jesus or to episodes recounting his activity. Thus, in the case of the "apocryphal" gospels, we are dealing with "creative reinterpretations" of the activity and teaching of Jesus as either continuations of the Gospels of the New Testament or as alternatives to them.

In the course of the first three centuries of Christianity, "authoritative" writings were distinguished from "disputed" and "rejected" (or "forged") writings. This development ultimately culminated in the contrast between "canonized" and "apocryphal" writings. This is first encountered in the thirty-ninth Easter Letter of Bishop Athanasius of Alexandria from 367 CE. Around the middle of the fourth century, the term "canon"—which had previously been used for the ecclesiastically valid statements of faith—established itself as a designation for the books that were to be read in the church, which were demarcated from writings that were designated as "non-canonical" or "apocryphal." This distinction was especially meant to regulate the reading of Christians—both in the church and also in private. According to Athanasius' letter, "apocryphal" writings should not be read in the church at all and in private only in exceptional cases.

Writings that could be brought into agreement with the basic convictions of Christianity—which were summarized in the "rule of faith," which could also be called "rule of truth" or "ecclesiastical rule"—were included in the Christian Bible. By contrast, writings for which this was, in the view of the ancient theologians mentioned above, not the case were rejected as "apocryphal" or "forged." These works also included the "apocryphal gospels." On the one hand, these works are known to us through references to them in the writings of early Christian theologians (sometimes they are mentioned only by their title and sometimes there are quotations from these writings). On the other hand, many of these works are known through numerous manuscripts that contain (often fragmentary) texts with "apocryphal" Jesus traditions.

In today's usage, "apocryphal gospels" is an umbrella term for a broad spectrum of texts. It designates not only the writings rejected by early Christian authors but more generally those Jesus traditions that are not found in the New Testament. These diverse texts did not form a corpus in antiquity, which is why it is misleading to refer to these works, as sometimes occurs, with designations such as "apocryphal Bible," "apocryphal New Testament," or "Bible of the heretics." Instead, "apocrypha of the New Testament" were first compiled in an edition by Johann Albert Fabricius in 1703 (second edition in 1719) with the title *Codex Apocryphus Novi Testamenti*. Here, "apocryphal" no longer meant "forged" or "heretical" writings. Instead, it meant writings that do not appear in the New Testament but are nevertheless of interest for the history of ancient Christianity. Since then, this usage has guided the investigation of these writings, which has resulted in numerous editions, translations, and studies (some of which can be found in the list of works at the end of the individual chapters of this book).

Editions of apocrypha of the New Testament or of ancient Christian apocrypha—and thus also of apocryphal gospels—can differ in content, depending on which writings are included in such a collection by the editors. The term "apocrypha" is usually retained, though not in the disparaging sense in which it is used by early Christian theologians. Sometimes the neutral designation "non-canonical" gospels is used. This describes the status of these texts in a way that is more impartial and, therefore, ultimately more appropriate. In any case, the expression "apocryphal" applies only to some of these texts, both in the meaning "hidden" and in the evaluation "forged" or "rejected." The *Gospel of Thomas*, the *Gospel of Judas*, the *Apocryphon of John*, and the *Apocryphon of James* do, in fact, designate themselves as "apocryphal"—i.e., as writings that require special insight to be understood. This is not, however, the case for other writings, such as the so-called Infancy Gospels, the *Gospel of Nicodemus*, and quite a few others. They were only designated as "apocryphal" in the disparaging sense later—i.e., they "became apocryphal" (on this, see the title of the work by Dieter Lührman in the list of resources at the end of this chapter).

Apocryphal gospels are thus important witnesses for the history of early Christianity—and then also for the history of the Middle Ages and of the modern period. They show that Christianity, reaching beyond the Gospels of the New Testament, has intensively occupied itself with the life of Jesus—with his birth and childhood, his family, his activity and teaching, his death and resurrection, and his appearances and instructions as the Risen One. Some of these works have had a deep impact upon the history of Christian piety. They have been translated into different languages, augmented, and presented in visual interpretations, such as mosaics and frescoes. By contrast, other apocryphal texts have disappeared from the Christian stream of tradition and have been rediscovered and published only in more recent times. In all their differences, the apocryphal gospels place the four Gospels that were included in the New Testament within a broader landscape of interpretations of the person of Jesus.

The apocryphal gospels provide important insights into the social history and history of piety of early Christianity. Some of these writings have had a significant impact upon how Jesus is viewed. At the same time, it must be kept in mind that only a few early Christian communities would have known—let alone possessed—all four of the Gospels that made it into the New Testament. Instead, it must be assumed that there were one or two of these Gospels in the communities, and beyond them, other writings, including works that are now assigned to the "apocryphal gospels." Some apocryphal texts are witnesses to Christian and "gnostic" groups in the environment of Christianity as it was developing into the great church. The investigation of the apocryphal gospels, therefore, expands our knowledge about early Christianity, both in terms of its interpretations of the person of Jesus and with respect to the use of writings in churches and in private contexts.

The Study of the Apocryphal Gospels

Until the last third of the nineteenth century, the apocryphal gospels were primarily known through references and quotations in the writings of early Christian theologians and through some manuscripts, especially the Infancy Gospels and the *Gospel of Nicodemus*. The aforementioned edition of Fabricius from 1703 lists ancient Christian references to these writings and provides Greek or Latin texts. Moreover, this edition includes a section titled "On the Sayings of Christ, our Savior, which are not contained in the Four Canonical Gospels" (*De Dictis Christi Servatoris Nostri: Quae in quatuor Evangeliis Canonicis non extant*).

Beyond this, numerous fragments with Jesus traditions—usually in Greek or Coptic—have been discovered in various locations. Some of these can be assigned to writings that were already known to us from references to apocryphal gospels in the writings of ancient Christian authors. In the case of quite a few of these fragments, however, it is not possible to provide a more precise specification of their content, length, or literary character. Finally, other writings are known to us only through quotations of ancient authors, though in some cases, the only information they provide is a title. All of these texts are readily accessible through editions, studies, and translations into modern European languages, such as English, French, Spanish, Dutch, and German. Moreover, there are quite a few introductory works that provide good overviews of these texts. As part of the Jesus tradition of early Christianity, the apocryphal gospels have also found a place in presentations of early Christian literature and the emergence of the New Testament canon. This has provided a far more multifaceted picture of the emergence of Christianity and its development in the first centuries.

INTRODUCTION

The Apocryphal Gospels and the Quest for the Historical Jesus

Do the apocryphal gospels contain distinctive traditions about the historical Jesus that are independent of the Gospels of the New Testament? Do they even result in a different picture of Jesus from the one that can be sketched on the basis of the New Testament Gospels and that has established itself in Christian tradition? These questions have received much discussion in scholarship. This discussion has been driven, not least, by the tantalizing possibility that previously unknown "hidden" writings could bring us closer to the person of Jesus and the content of his activity and teaching. Already in the eighteenth century, the Enlightenment thinker Gotthold Ephraim Lessing (in *Neue Hypothese über die Evangelisten als bloss menschliche Geschichtsschreiber betrachtet*) had speculated that a "Gospel of the Nazarenes," which contained the oldest reports of the teaching and life of Jesus, lay behind the New Testament Gospels. The discovery of numerous apocryphal texts since the end of the nineteenth century gave new impetus to the idea that through apocryphal texts one could obtain new information about Jesus that the New Testament does not contain or even perhaps consciously keeps quiet. In some corners of North American scholarship, a view of Jesus that takes its orientation from the Jesus tradition of the New Testament is sometimes replaced by a one-sided privileging of the apocryphal texts, which allegedly contain old Jesus traditions that are independent of the New Testament Gospels. In the meantime, this sometimes naïve enthusiasm for the apocryphal gospels has given way to their sober historical placement in the history of Christianity.

The question of whether or not a writing made its way into the New Testament cannot, of course, answer the question of its historical value or of the age of the traditions contained within it. What an early Christian text contributes to the reconstruction of the activity and fate of Jesus is, therefore, independent of whether it is a "canonical" or "apocryphal" text. Apocryphal texts can contain historically reliable information and, conversely, New Testament texts contain legendary traditions that contribute nothing or only very little to the historical quest for Jesus (for example the narratives about the birth and childhood of Jesus in Matthew and Luke). In any case, the question of the historical value of the apocryphal texts cannot be answered in a sweeping manner but only with respect to each text on its own. Nevertheless, the previously mentioned testimonies of early Christian authors indicate that apocryphal gospels came into view later than the Gospels that were included in the New Testament and were then set over against these or measured by them. Accordingly, it seems that the Four Gospels, which would later represent the testimony of Jesus in the New Testament, had already gained acceptance in Christian communities before other gospels came into view.

In some cases, it is indeed possible—sometimes even probable—that apocryphal writings contain old Jesus traditions. We owe, however, the narrative framework in which these traditions are embedded to the Gospels that were included in the New Testament, which recount the activity of Jesus in Galilee and Jerusalem. This does not represent a value judgment about the apocryphal gospels. Their significance for the history of Christianity does not, however, reside in the bringing to light of new historical insights about Jesus. Rather, they are important witnesses to the variety of interpretations of Jesus and the social and cultural world of ancient Christianity.

Sources and Studies

Bockmuehl, Markus. *Ancient Apocryphal Gospels*. Louisville: Westminster John Knox, 2017.

Bovon, François, Pierre Geoltrain, and Jean-Daniel Kaestli, eds. *Écrits apocryphes chrétiens*. 2 vols. Bibliothèque de la Pléiade 442 and 516. Paris: Gallimard, 1997/2005.

Burke, Tony, and Brent Landau, eds. *New Testament Apocrypha: More Noncanonical Scriptures*. 2 vols. Grand Rapids: Eerdmans, 2016/2020.

Cartlidge, David R., and J. Keith Elliott. *Art and the Christian Apocrypha*. London: Routledge, 2001.

Ehrman, Bart D., and Zlatko Pleše, eds. and trans. *The Apocryphal Gospels: Texts and Translations*. Oxford: Oxford University Press, 2011.

Elliott, J. K., ed. *The Apocryphal Jesus: Legends of the Early Church*. Oxford: Oxford University Press, 1996.

———, trans. *The Apocryphal New Testament: A Collection of Apocryphal Christian Literature in an English Translation*. Oxford: Oxford University Press, 1993. Rev. reprint, 1999.

Fabricius, Johann Albert, ed. *Codex apocryphus Novi Testamenti*. 2 vols. Hamburg: Benjamin Schiller, 1703. 2nd ed., 1719.

Foster, Paul, ed. *The Non-Canonical Gospels*. London: T. & T. Clark, 2008.

Holmes, Michael E., ed. and trans. *The Apostolic Fathers*. Grand Rapids: Baker, 1999.

Klauck. Hans-Josef. *Apocryphal Gospels: An Introduction*. Translated by Brian McNeil. London: T. & T. Clark, 2003.

Lessing, Gotthold Ephraim. *Neue Hypothese über die Evangelisten als bloss menschliche Geschichtsschreiber betrachtet*. Wolfenbüttel, 1778. Reprinted in Gotthold Ephraim

INTRODUCTION

Lessing. *Werke*, vol. 7, edited by Herbert G. Göpfert et al., 614–36. 8 vols. Munich: Hanser, 1970–1979.

Lienhard, Joseph T., trans. *Origen: Homilies on Luke, Fragments of Luke*. Fathers of the Church 94. Washington, DC: Catholic University of America Press, 1996.

Lührmann, Dieter. *Die apokryph gewordenen Evangelien Studien zu neuen Texten und zu neuen Fragen*. Novum Testamentum Supplements 112. Leiden: Brill, 2004.

Markschies, Christoph and Jens Schröter, eds. *Antike christliche Apokryphen in deutscher Übersetzung*. I Band: *Evangelien und Verwandtes*. Tübingen: Mohr/Siebeck, 2012.

Meyer, Marvin, ed. *The Nag Hammadi Scriptures: The International Edition*. New York: HarperOne, 2007.

Otero, Aurelio de Santos. *Los Evangelios Apócrifos. Edición crítica y bilingüe*. Madrid: Biblioteca de Autores Cristianos, 2006.

Schneemelcher, Wilhelm, ed. *New Testament Apocrypha*. 2 vols. Translated by R. McL. Wilson. Rev. ed. Louisville: Westminster John Knox, 1991/1992.

Schröter, Jens, ed. *The Apocryphal Gospels within the Context of Early Christian Theology*. BETL 260. Leuven: Peeters, 2013.

Schröter, Jens, and Christine Jacobi, eds. *From Thomas to Tertullian: Christian Literary Receptions of Jesus in the Second and Third Centuries CE*. Vol. 2 of *The Reception of Jesus in the First Three Centuries*. Edited by Chris Keith et al. London: T. & T. Clark, 2020.

Thilo, Johann Karl, ed. *Codex apocryphus Novi Testamenti*. Leipzig: Vogel, 1832

Tischendorf, Constantin von, ed. *Evangelia Apocrypha*. Leipzig: Mendelsohn, 1853. 2nd ed., 1876.

Watson, Francis. *Gospel Writing: A Canonical Perspective*. Grand Rapids: Eerdmans, 2013.

Wayment, Thomas A., ed. *The Text of the New Testament Apocrypha (100–400 CE)*. London: T. & T. Clark, 2013.

Williamson, Geoffrey A., trans. *Eusebius: The History of the Church from Christ to Constantine*. Rev. ed. by Andrew Louth. London: Penguin, 1989.

2

"Infancy Gospels"

Narratives about the Birth and Childhood of Jesus

Introduction

STORIES ABOUT THE BIRTH and childhood of Jesus occur in only two of the Gospels of the New Testament: Matthew and Luke. The Gospel of Mark, by contrast, starts with the appearance of John the Baptist. The Gospel of John begins with a prologue about the "Word" (Logos), which was already with God before the creation of the world and then became flesh in Jesus Christ.

In the birth narratives of Matthew and Luke we are dealing with legendary traditions that interpret the birth of Jesus brought about by the Holy Spirit as the fulfillment of prophetic promises and as the saving action of God for his people Israel. Thus, from a historical perspective, nothing can be derived from the New Testament Gospels about the time before the public appearance of Jesus. While the stories in Matthew and Luke agree in some points (for example in specifying Mary and Joseph as the parents of Jesus, in the birth of Jesus in Bethlehem, and in the mention of King Herod), they otherwise present the birth of Jesus and the accompanying circumstances differently. The Gospel of Matthew begins with a genealogy that traces back the origin of Jesus to Abraham and places special emphasis on the fact that he comes from the line of David. It then recounts the coming of magi from the east to Jerusalem, Herod's massacre of the children, the flight of Joseph and Mary with the child

Jesus to Egypt, their return, and, finally, the move to Nazareth. In Luke the births of John the Baptist and Jesus are announced by the angel Gabriel and then narrated in succession. Mary and Joseph also have to travel from Nazareth to Bethlehem, where Jesus is born and laid in a manger. The birth of Jesus is praised in songs by Zechariah, the father of John, by Mary, and by the aged Simeon, and proclaimed by angels to shepherds in the fields as the coming of the Savior. Finally, Luke recounts the presentation of Jesus as well as the episode of the twelve-year-old Jesus, who enters into a discussion with the teachers of Israel in the Jerusalem temple. This is the only episode in the New Testament about the childhood of Jesus before his public appearance.

Starting in the second century, other writings about the birth and childhood of Jesus emerged. Scholars refer to them as Infancy Gospels. They continue the tendency of narrating the birth and childhood of Jesus in a legendary way. This met the need of reporting more about the early period of Jesus' life than what is found in the Gospels of Matthew and Luke. Thus, these texts serve to illustrate the miraculous birth of Jesus and the extraordinary abilities that he already possessed as a child. In this way, they also reinforce the confession of Jesus as the incarnate Son of God and defend it against doubt among insiders and polemic from outsiders.

While the Infancy Gospels do not increase our historical knowledge about Jesus, they do play an important role for the history of Christian piety. The legends about the circumstances of the birth of Jesus, episodes from the childhood of Jesus, and stories about his parents have often been handed down, embellished, and presented in pictorial form. Thus, from an early period onward, the Infancy Gospels and related texts about Mary, Joseph, and John the Baptist have been a firm component of the Jesus tradition of Christianity to such an extent that "canonical" and "apocryphal" traditions could seamlessly merge into one another.

The beginnings of the Infancy Gospels reach back into the second century CE. In the course of their transmission they were combined with one another and enriched with other stories. Most of these writings are connected therefore, literarily and in their transmission history. In what follows we will first introduce the two oldest Infancy Gospels and then look at their reception and influence (*Rezeptions- und Wirkungsgeschichte*) in a few later writings.

The *Protevangelium of James*

The writing known by the title *Protevangelium of James* is the earliest and most influential Infancy Gospel. The earliest reference to this work is found in Origen's commentary on Matthew, which was written around 230 CE. Here, Origen speaks of a "book of James," which says that the brothers of Jesus mentioned in Matthew 13:55 are sons of Joseph from a marriage prior to his marriage with Mary (*Comm. Matt.* 10.17). Origen apparently refers here to the *Protevangelium*, where this interpretation appears (9:2; 17:1; 18:1). Prior to Origen, we find the statement that Mary's virginity was validated even after the birth of Jesus in Clement of Alexandria (*Strom.* 7.93.7). Since the episode in question likewise appears in the *Protevangelium* (chaps. 19–20), it is possible that Clement knew this work.

Beyond this, there are additional connections between the *Protevangelium of James* and comments made by early Christian theologians. In his *Dialogue with Trypho*, which was written around the middle of the second century CE, Justin notes that Jesus was born in a cave, since Joseph could not find a place to stay in Bethlehem (78.5). There is also talk of Jesus being born in a cave in the *Protevangelium* (first mentioned in 18:1) but not in Matthew or Luke. Justin's statement, however, need not necessarily go back to a knowledge of the *Protevangelium*. It is also possible that Justin was the source for the *Protevangelium* or—and this is more probable—that we are dealing with a tradition that the two works took up independently. This view is supported by the fact that, in the relevant section, Justin freely summarizes traditions about the birth of Jesus from Matthew and Luke, and that the *Protevangelium* likewise incorporates diverse traditions surrounding the birth of Jesus. In other words, both authors are making liberal use of pre-existing traditions. In his work *Scorpiace* (*Antidote for the Scorpion's Sting*), composed around 211/212 CE, the theologian and lawyer Tertullian mentions the tradition of the death of a certain Zechariah (*Scorp.* 8). The *Protevangelium* concludes with an account of the death of Zechariah, the father of John the Baptist (23–24). However, it is not necessary to conclude from this that Tertullian knew the *Protevangelium*, since he could be referencing the tradition of the martyrdom of the Jewish prophet Zechariah that is attested in Matthew 23:35//Luke 11:51.

Thus, the early Christian witnesses indicate that the *Protevangelium* is situated in the context of traditions about the birth of Jesus that are known by Christian authors in the second century CE. Moreover, it combines stories from the Gospels of Matthew and Luke. It follows from this that the *Protevangelium* was presumably composed in the later part of the second century CE.

The *Protevangelium* is preserved in more than 140 Greek manuscripts and in numerous translations into Syriac, Coptic, Georgian, Armenian, Ethiopic, and Arabic. The large number of Church Slavic manuscripts is also notable. In addition, a fragmentary Latin translation has been preserved. The writing thus enjoyed great popularity in the churches of the East. In the Western church, by contrast, it was rejected and was accordingly largely unknown up to and into the sixteenth century. The reason for this was the previously mentioned view that the brothers of Jesus were the sons of Joseph from an earlier marriage. By contrast, the Western church held the view (first espoused by Jerome) that the brothers and sisters mentioned in the New Testament were male and female cousins of Jesus. The title *Protevangelium of James* is first encountered in the Latin translation of the French humanist Guillaume Postel published in 1522 in Basel. It goes back to Postel's speculation that the writing represents the lost first part of the Gospel of Mark, which begins with the appearance of John the Baptist and, therefore, was preceded by a "Protevangelium" ("First Gospel"). Postel had come to know the writing in the East and made it known in the Western church through his translation. The translation was printed—alongside the Greek text—by Fabricius in his *Codex Apocryphus Novi Testamenti*. Fabricius is also responsible for the division of the work into 25 chapters, which is still common today.

The oldest title preserved in a manuscript (Papyrus Bodmer V, from the fourth century) is quite different: "The Birth of Mary, The Revelation of James." With the ascription to James the work is attributed to a fictive author who takes the floor at the end of the writing: "But I, James, the one who has written this account . . ." (25:1). The person who is meant is the brother of Jesus who must belong to the mentioned sons of Joseph from his first marriage and who thus wrote down the story later. We are dealing here with a fictive ascription, for this work could not have been written by a brother of Jesus. In some manuscripts the writing also has other titles, which usually emphasize the role of Mary as "God-bearer" (*theotokos*). In this way, they more fittingly express the content of the work than the designation *Protevangelium*, for the work deals, to a considerable extent, with the birth and childhood of Mary, her marriage and pregnancy, and then with the birth of Jesus and its accompanying circumstances, in which the continuing virginity of Mary, even after the birth, plays an important role.

A critical edition of the Greek text was provided by Constantin von Tischendorf in his collection of apocryphal gospels. A revised new edition that takes into account the subsequently discovered Greek manuscripts (including Papyrus Bodmer V) was published along with a French translation by Émile de Strycker in 1961. More recent translations (such as those of Ronald Hock, Gerhard Schneider, Lily Vuong, and Bart Ehrman) are based on these editions. We do not yet have a critical edition of the text that takes into account all the known Greek manuscripts (the most recent fragment to become known, a piece from a papyrus codex of the fourth century, was published by Alex Ladenheim and Thomas Wayment in 2011) as well as the ancient translations mentioned above.

Traces of reworkings can already be identified in the manuscript tradition. In chapter 18:2 the narrative suddenly changes to the first person singular. This marks the beginning of a passage that is introduced with "But I, Joseph" and that reaches to 19:1. The section describes how Joseph, who has gone in search of a midwife, experiences the whole world standing still at the time of Jesus' birth, which simultaneously takes place in the cave. Those who are eating stop in the middle of the movement and look up into the sky; even the birds in flight stop without movement. Everything that lives freezes for a moment. Here, for the portrayal of the birth of Jesus, the author makes use of a motif that is frequently attested in antiquity and in the modern period: The birth is not narrated directly but the event is portrayed from the perspective of Joseph, who experiences this moment as one that has special significance for all of creation, without him knowing about the birth that is taking place at this point in time. Instead of this passage, the fourth-century Papyrus Bodmer V contains only a short note that recounts how Joseph finds a Hebrew midwife whom he had left Mary to seek. Later textual witnesses and some translations present the vision, by contrast, in the third person.

Another discrepancy within the textual tradition concerns the testing of Mary's virginity after the birth of Jesus (chap. 20). After the midwife Salome expresses doubt, she tests Mary's virginity herself. Her hand is then consumed by fire and threatens to fall off. In response to this, she confesses her unbelief and invokes the God of Israel in prayer, whom she has always faithfully served. An angel of the Lord announces to her that her prayer has been heard and that she will be healed; then, she may take the newborn king of Israel in her arm. This episode appears in a shorter version in Papyrus Bodmer V; this manuscript also lacks the encounter between Herod and the magi in chapter 21. By contrast, the view that the murder of Zechariah is a later addition, as is sometimes assumed, cannot be verified, as it does occur in the Bodmer papyrus.

Thus, the textual tradition of the *Protevangelium* indicates a certain fluidity. Irrespective of this, it is clear that we are dealing with a narrative that has combined the traditions about the birth of Jesus, including those that we find in Matthew and Luke, with a story about the birth and childhood of Mary, which is placed before the birth Jesus.

The narrative of the *Protevangelium* reflects the milieu of the story of Israel. At the beginning we find the portrayal of Joachim and Anna, the parents of Mary, who are mentioned here for the first time in Christian literature. They are portrayed as a well-to-do, older Israelite couple who are grieving over the fact that they do not have a child. Their introduction is followed by Anna's prayer that God would end her barrenness. Here, a clear connection to the story of the birth of Samuel in 1 Samuel 1 is established. His mother is also called Anna (or Hannah), and his birth also occurs only after a long period of childlessness and in response to the mother's lament; in addition, both Annas promise to devote their child to the Lord after its birth. The birth of Mary is then announced to Anna by an angel of the Lord, and it is noted—after the fact—that this had also already been communicated to Joachim by an angel. Here, it is disputed whether Mary is conceived in the *Protevangelium* in a natural way or whether a conception through the divine Spirit is in view. The decision depends on whether Joachim is informed by an angel that Anna *has* conceived in her body or that she *will* conceive (4:2) and whether Anna, shortly thereafter, says to Joachim that she *has* already conceived or that she *will* conceive (4:4). Both readings are attested by manuscripts. Based on the flow of the argument, the future form is more likely, since it takes up the announcement of the angel to Anna. Moreover, a supernatural conception of Mary is unlikely in light of the connection to 1 Samuel 1. What is meant to be emphasized is the fact that God can also bring an end to long periods of childlessness and can give older couples the blessing of children. At any rate, there can be no talk of a "virginal conception," for Joachim and Anna have already been a married couple for a long time and are presented as grieving over the fact that they are still childless. Accordingly, the *Protevangelium* cannot be claimed as a witness for the notion of a virgin birth (or the "immaculate conception") of Mary, even though the text has often been understood in this way.

After her birth and a time spent in her parents' house, Mary, in fulfillment of Anna's vows, is brought into the temple, where she lives until she is twelve, when she is to be married according to the instruction of the angel. Joseph comes into view for the first time in chapter 9. According to a decision determined by a sign arranged by the angel of the Lord (a dove flies out of Joseph's rod and onto his head), he is shown to be the chosen husband for Mary. Joseph, however, objects that he already has sons and that he is already old, whereas Mary is a young girl. At this point, we find the aforementioned statement about the sons of Joseph. On the basis of the priest's warning not to oppose God, Joseph does then take Mary to himself. Chapter 10 recounts that Mary works on the curtain for the Jerusalem temple as a virgin. The scene was also presented iconographically at an early date, for example, in the mosaics of the triumphal arch of Santa Maria Maggiore in Rome from the fifth century CE. Moreover, in this context we encounter the important information that Mary belongs to the line of David. In distinction from what we find in the Gospel of Matthew, where Joseph is placed in the genealogy of David (1:16; found also in Luke 3:31), here Mary belongs in the Davidic line of descent.

On the way to the well to fetch water, Mary meets an angel who ceremoniously greets her ("Greetings, you who are favored! The Lord is with you. You are blessed among women," 11:1; cf. Luke 1:28, 42) and announces to her that she will conceive through the Word of God. This is described in a combination of Luke 1:35 and Matthew 1:18: "The power of God will overshadow you. Therefore the holy one born from you will be called the Son of the Highest. And you will name him Jesus, for he will save his people from their sins" (11:3). After this, Mary's visit to her relative Elizabeth is recounted (12:2–3; cf. Luke 1:39–45). When Joseph notices the pregnancy, he is troubled and suspects that Mary has betrayed him. As in the Gospel of Matthew, however, it is explained to him in a dream that Mary's pregnancy was brought about by the Holy Spirit (13–14; cf. Matthew 1:19–24). After this, the priests also become convinced that Mary and Joseph have not violated Mary's virginity (15–16).

Starting in chapter 17, the focus is directed to the birth of Jesus. Here, traditions from Matthew and Luke are interwoven with one another. This chapter begins with Augustus' order that the inhabitants of Bethlehem register themselves in Judaea—an idiosyncratic reception of Luke 2:1, where this order applies to the whole inhabited world. This is presumably caused by the fact that from the beginning onward, the events in the *Protevangelium* and in Matthew take place in Judea, but the author wanted to connect it to the story of the journey to Bethlehem from the Gospel of Luke, where Mary and Joseph live in Nazareth. Chapter 18 portrays their arrival in the previously mentioned cave and Joseph's experience of the world standing still during the birth of Jesus. Chapters 19–20 deal with the testing of Mary's virginity by Salome and her repentance of her unbelief.

Chapters 21–24 present a larger narrative complex, whose framework is formed by the homage of the magi and Herod's massacre of the children. Thus, this section represents a reworking of the story from Matthew 2, embellished by material featuring John the Baptist and his parents Elizabeth and Zechariah. After Herod recognizes that the magi have returned to their land by another way, he arranges for the massacre of the children. Mary hides Jesus in a manger. By contrast, Elizabeth flees into the mountains with her child John, where a mountain receives her and she is protected by an angel of the Lord. Herod wants to learn from Zechariah where his son is hidden and has him killed when he refuses to provide this information. Zechariah is succeeded as high priest by Simeon, who is also mentioned in Luke 2:25–35 at the presentation of Jesus at the temple.

The *Protevangelium* has a clear interest in Mary, the mother of Jesus. She is consecrated to God even before her birth, blessed multiple times by the priests, lives in a sanctuary already in her parents' house (cf. the "sanctuary in the bedroom" mentioned in 6:1), and her purity and virginity are emphasized even after the birth of Jesus. Nevertheless, the *Protevangelium* should not be designated as a "Mariological writing." The narrative of Mary is located within the broader horizon of the story that begins with Joachim and Anna and leads to the birth of Jesus. In the process, alongside the orientation to Mary, the story of the virginal birth of Jesus and the subsequent persecutions by Herod come into view. The *Protevangelium* could have been composed, therefore, in order to safeguard the early Christian tradition of the virginal birth of Jesus, which was called into question by both Jewish and gentile opponents. The earliest reference to a rumor that Mary was raped by the Roman soldier Panthera and that the resulting pregnancy was hidden by the legend of the virgin birth occurs in Origen's writing *Against Celsus*. Origen reports that the second-century philosopher Celsus accused the Christians of having invented the tale of a virgin birth of Jesus, hiding that Mary was in fact convicted of adultery and expelled by Joseph (*Cels*. 1:18, 32). Against such polemics the *Protevangelium* presents a story that defends the virginity of

Mary in a thoroughgoing way and even expands this beyond the birth of Jesus (a notion that does not occur in the New Testament). The persecutions that begin after the birth of Jesus and the martyrdom of Zechariah could also point to the hostilities against Christians at the hands of the authorities of the Roman empire.

The *Protevangelium* had an extensive impact, both in terms of its literary reception and in art and piety. The veneration of the holy Anna, which finds expression both in the churches dedicated to her and in the medieval depictions of Virgin and Child with Saint Anne ("Anna Selbdritt"), is based on the *Protevangelium*. This is closely connected with the tradition of the virginal conception of Mary. While there is no explicit mention of this in the *Protevangelium*, the text has often been understood in this way and has contributed to the notion of the "immaculate conception" (*immaculata conceptio*), which is celebrated in an ecclesiastical high festival on December 8 and was even elevated to the rank of a dogma in the Roman Catholic Church in 1854. The tradition of the birth of Jesus in a cave is also developed narratively for the first time in the *Protevangelium*. Subsequently, it has often been presented pictorially. In Bethlehem, under the Church of the Nativity, a cave marked by a star, in which Jesus is said to have been born, is still shown today. The episode of the rescuing of John from Herod's massacre of the children appears on a mosaic from the fifth century in the church of Santa Maria Maggiore in Rome. Finally, the tradition of the presentation of Mary in the temple (celebrated on November 21) as well as the designation of Mary as "God-bearer" is also connected with the *Protevangelium*. While this title does not occur in the writing itself, it was brought into connection with the text, as can be seen not least through the titles that have been assigned to it. Finally, the *Protevangelium* was taken up and developed further in later Infancy Gospels. We will return to this point below.

The *Infancy Gospel of Thomas*

Another early Infancy Gospel is associated with the name of the apostle Thomas (the *Gospel of Thomas* from Nag Hammadi is a different writing, which we will discuss later). He is introduced at the beginning of the work as "Thomas, the Israelite." This text is also known by the name *Paidika* ("Childhood Deeds"), which occurs in the title of some manuscripts and is probably the original title of the work. *Infancy Thomas* has a fundamentally different character from the *Protevangelium*. It narrates loosely linked episodes from the childhood of Jesus, beginning when Jesus is five years old and ending with the story of the twelve-year-old Jesus at the temple in Jerusalem (cf. Luke 2:42–51). Like the *Protevangelium*, *Infancy Thomas* goes back in its basic form to the second century. The earliest reference to it could be in Irenaeus. In his dispute with a group called the Marcosians, he mentions a "forged story" drawn upon by them, according to which the Lord, when he was still a child, exhorted his teacher, from whom he learned the letters, to explain to him the meaning of the Alpha before he gave him information about what the Beta is (*Haer.* 1.20.1). This episode has points of contact with *Infancy Thomas* 6. There, Jesus asks his teacher Zachaeus, who teaches him all the letters, how he could teach others the Beta when he does not even know the Alpha. After this, Jesus teaches Zachaeus before many hearers about the form of the letter Alpha. Another parallel appears in chapter 4 of the *Epistle of the Apostles* (on this, see the discussion in chap. 5 below). It is possible that this episode should be understood as a parody of a situation from school instruction that is meant to highlight the cleverness of the child Jesus. We need not necessarily conclude from this that *Infancy Thomas* is known by Irenaeus or by the *Epistle of the Apostles*. We could also be dealing with an orally transmitted story that has been independently taken up by various writings.

The tradition history of *Infancy Thomas* is extremely complex. Accordingly, it will scarcely be possible to reconstruct an original version of the text. We must reckon with diverse expansions and revisions, through which a basic literary layer—presumably consisting of chapters 2–9, 11–16, and 19 (as in the earliest versions)—was enriched with additional episodes. The versions of *Infancy Thomas* most well-known today go back to the edition of Tischendorf, who had divided the manuscripts into a longer recension with 19 chapters and a shorter recension with 11 chapters. The original language was presumably Greek, though a Syriac original has also been postulated.

The oldest preserved Greek manuscript is Sabaiticus 259 (named after the Monastery of Mar Saba, where it resides) from the eleventh century. This version of the text was edited by Tony Burke and appears also in a translation by Reidar Aasgaard. Most of the Greek manuscripts date from the fourteenth to the sixteenth centuries. Some translations, however, are older. A Latin manuscript comes from the fifth century and three Syriac manuscripts from the fifth or sixth century. According to

Tony Burke, who has published a critical edition of the Syriac tradition of *Infancy Thomas*, the Syriac text best preserves the earliest form of the text. The Latin text is also found incorporated in a number of manuscripts of the so-called *Gospel of Pseudo-Matthew* (on this, see below). Other translations are extant in Church Slavic, Ethiopic, Arabic, Georgian, Old Irish, and a second, longer Latin version. Some of the manuscripts come from a later period, and the relationship to the older manuscripts cannot always be clarified with certainty. The tradition history of *Infancy Thomas* thus shows that the work enjoyed great popularity in different Christian cultures. It was handed down in different versions, translated into diverse languages, and reworked in later Infancy Gospels. A very impressive pictorial representation of the childhood stories is preserved in the *Klosterneuburger Evangelienwerk* from the fourteenth century.

In the Greek manuscripts, Thomas is mentioned as the author of the work, sometimes with the additions "the Israelite," "the Israelite Philosopher," or "the Holy Apostle." The apostle Thomas is also the pseudonymous author behind two works from Codex II of the Nag Hammadi Library, namely, the *Gospel of Thomas* and the *Book of Thomas the Contender* (or Athlete).

The content of *Infancy Thomas* consists of loosely linked episodes in which astonishing miracles of the child Jesus are recounted. The longer text published by Tischendorf begins with Jesus making sparrows fashioned from mud fly (chap. 2). Then he causes a boy with whom he is upset to wither (3). He causes another boy in the village who struck him on the shoulder to fall dead (4). When Joseph rebukes him for this, he causes the people who had told his father about his deeds to go blind. Chapters 6–8 recount the story of the teacher Zacchaeus who wants to teach Jesus the alphabet, but is abruptly attacked by him as a hypocrite and is humbled by Jesus' superior knowledge. After this, Zacchaeus gives up his attempt, declaring that Jesus is something great, "whether a divine being or an angel—I do not know even what to say" (7:4). In response, Jesus laughs, heals all the people whom he had previously cursed, and reveals that he has "come from above" to call people "to the realm above" (8:1).

In the following chapters, the character of the rather offensive episodes (in which Jesus miraculously harms other children) changes to miracles of healing and other helpful deeds of Jesus. He raises a young man who died when he fell off a roof (9) and heals a man who had injured himself with an axe and was bleeding to death (10). Jesus carries water home to his mother, although the jug is shattered (11) and ensures an astonishing yield when he helps his father to sow wheat in their field (12). In the last two miracles, his age is specified as six and eight years. In chapters 14 and 15, other episodes are recounted about Jesus and teachers, whom he once again outclasses through his wisdom. Three healings or raisings of the dead follow in chapters 16–18 before the narrative circle closes with the episode of the twelve-year-old Jesus in the Jerusalem temple taken from the Gospel of Luke.

Infancy Thomas is obviously interested in extending the narrative of the divine character of the child Jesus, inspired by Luke 2:42–51, into his early childhood. While scholars have often shown irritation over the banality and perceived offensiveness of these episodes, it should not be overlooked that we are dealing with an ancient "biographical" writing that presupposes the New Testament Gospels—at least the Gospel of Luke and the Gospel of John—and wishes to supplement or expand a particular aspect of its subject, namely, the divine wisdom and authority that could be perceived in Jesus from early on. The features of *Infancy Thomas*'s picture of Jesus that appear arbitrary and aggressive can be explained by the fact that Jesus is presented as a child here. But his healing and helping activity as well as his teaching in the Holy Spirit are also emphasized. These actions point forward to his later activity, which is presupposed rather than narrated in *Infancy Thomas*.

The Further Development of the Infancy Gospels

In later Infancy Gospels the events around the birth and childhood of Jesus were developed and further embellished. Here, the two oldest texts—the *Protevangelium* and *Infancy Thomas*—are enriched with additional episodes about miraculous occurrences and connected to larger narratives. The relevant manuscripts exist in different languages, with it often being impossible to specify exactly the date and original language of the respective writings.

The *Arabic Infancy Gospel* has been published in two forms. The first, published from a fifteenth-century manuscript by Heinrich Sike in 1697, includes a good portion of *Infancy Thomas*. The second, published in 1973 by Mario E. Provera comes from a manuscript dated 1299; it lacks the Infancy Thomas material and is likely closer to the original form of the text. That same form is found also incorporated in a Syriac work called "The History of the Blessed Virgin Mary." This was edited in 1899 by Sir Ernest Alfred Wallis Budge. The gospel presumably arose in the sixth century, perhaps in Syriac, and was then translated into Arabic.

In the first section (chaps. 1–41 in Sike's numbering) the two versions mostly agree with each other. Using the birth stories of Matthew and Luke as well as the *Protevangelium* 1–9, they recount the birth of Jesus in Bethlehem as well as episodes known from other writings, such as the shepherds in the field, the coming of the magi, and the anger of Herod. Another complex is devoted to the family's journey to Egypt (chaps. 10–24). Mary plays an important role in the miracles that take place on the way. Among other things, the family meets two robbers about whom Jesus prophesies that they will be crucified with him in Jerusalem in thirty years. In Sike's version of the text, the three-year stay in Egypt is mentioned summarily in chapter 25 and concludes with the note that Jesus performed many miracles in Egypt, "which can be found neither in the Infancy Gospel nor in the complete Gospel." This apparently alludes to an earlier Infancy Gospel, maybe to the Syriac source of the text or the *Protevangelium*. The "complete Gospel" could also refer to the Gospel Harmony of Tatian (the *Diatessaron*), which was part of the New Testament in place of the four Gospels in the Syrian sphere until the fifth century CE.

After the return from Egypt, Joseph, as in the Gospel of Matthew, immediately receives the command to go to Nazareth and to remain there (26). The following episodes occur, however, in Bethlehem and its surroundings, where additional miracles take place (chs. 27–35). Beginning in chapter 36, Nazareth is then presupposed as the location of the events. Episodes from the childhood of Jesus are now recounted. Some of the miracles (including a story in which Jesus encounters a dyer and another in which several children proclaim him a king) are found in the *Armenian Infancy Gospel* and likely draw on a common pool of childhood stories. In the latter part (chaps. 42–50), the two versions deviate from each other. While Sike's manuscript provides pieces from *Infancy Thomas*, Provera's manuscript contains a number of episodes from the New Testament Gospels and Acts.

The *Gospel of Pseudo-Matthew* is another reworking of the *Protevangelium*. It was composed in Latin and can probably be dated to around the middle of the seventh century CE. The title comes from Tischendorf, who took his orientation from a fictive epistolary correspondence between Jerome and the bishops Chromatius and Heliodorus, though it now appears that this exchange was appended to the work at a later time.

"INFANCY GOSPELS"

The work that follows is introduced as a translation into Latin of the Gospel of Matthew composed in Hebrew, specifically of the part about the birth and childhood of Jesus. In this way, an old tradition that the Gospel of Matthew was written in Hebrew is related to the story that follows about the birth and childhood of Jesus (which was not, of course, part of the Gospel of Matthew) and authorized through the alleged translation of Jerome.

The first edition of the text was produced in 1832 by Johann Karl Thilo on the basis of a Parisian manuscript from the fourteenth century. This version is basically a revision of the *Protevangelium*. Tischendorf based his edition of 1851 (revised in 1876) on four manuscripts, three of which incorporate *Infancy Thomas*. Tischendorf regarded this as an original part of the *Pseudo-Matthew* and attached it to his edition as the "Pars Altera" or "second part" (numbered as chaps. 25–42). This expanded form of the text was handed down in numerous medieval manuscripts, becoming a means of transmitting the *Infancy Thomas* stories to the West. A recent translation of the text by Brandon Hawk includes the Pars altera along with additional stories found in other *Pseudo-Matthew* manuscripts. Jan Gijsel describes 190 manuscripts of the text in his 1997 critical edition, and more have been found in the years since.

Pseudo-Matthew originally began with a prologue that traced back the work to James, the son of Joseph the carpenter. This already signals a connection to the *Protevangelium* (which, as noted above, closes with an attribution to James). In its first part (1–17), the story of the birth of Mary and her youth is recounted. Here, some features of the *Protevangelium* are revised. For example, Anna gives birth after nine months instead of the seven mentioned in the *Protevangelium*. Moreover, it can be seen that the narrative of the *Protevangelium*, which is embedded in a Jewish milieu, is now placed in a different context. Connections can be seen to ascetic and monastic traditions, such as when Mary's life in the temple, where she lives from the age of three to fourteen, is portrayed in analogy to monastic life (in 6:2 her daily routine is presented in detail with a specification of the hours) or when she professes her commitment to lifelong chastity—possibly an allusion to the rule of Benedict. Moreover, going beyond the *Protevangelium*, the virginity of Mary after the birth is explicitly confirmed by two midwives: Salome and the newly-introduced Zahel. Finally, the tradition of the ox and donkey at the manger appears for the first time in *Pseudo-Matthew* (14:1). This is grounded with two sayings from the prophets: "The ox knows its owner, and the donkey its master's crib" (Isa 1:3) and "In the middle of two animals you will be recognized" (Hab 3:2; in the Greek and Latin versions).

The following section of the text (chaps. 18–24) features several episodes that are said to have taken place on Mary and Joseph's journey with Jesus to Egypt. The family encounters a number of wild animals, and even some dragons, who are all tamed by the infant Jesus. Thus, the end-time peace is realized on the way, as it was prophesied by the prophet Isaiah: "The wolf and the lamb shall feed together, the lion shall eat straw like the ox" (Isa 65:25). When the family rests because Mary is exhausted from the heat, a palm bends down at the word of the small child Jesus to offer his mother its fruit. When Mary enters an Egyptian temple with Jesus, the 365 idols that are there collapse. This is also grounded with a prophetic saying ("Behold, the Lord will come upon a swift cloud and all of the graven images of Egypt will be shaken by his presence," Isa 19:1).

Pseudo-Matthew expands on traditions about Mary and about Jesus and his parents' journey to Egypt. Like the *Arabic Infancy Gospel*, it represents a continuation of already existing writings, which it augments through additional traditions. It is thus a witness to the fact that the traditions about Mary, about the birth of Jesus, and related episodes were cultivated and handed down in Christian contexts, and in this case specifically in ascetic, monastic contexts.

Another Latin Infancy Gospel, called the *Book about the Birth of the Savior*, became known through the publication of two manuscripts—Arundel 404 and Codex Hereford (fourteenth or thirteenth century, both in England)—by M. R. James in 1927. A number of additional manuscripts have been found since James produced his edition; the oldest dates from the beginning of the ninth century. These "Latin Infancy Gospels," as he called them, feature a combination of the *Protevangelium* (which it evidently knows in a Latin translation), *Pseudo-Matthew*, and an otherwise lost Infancy Gospel (called the *Liber de nativitate Salvatoris*, or *Book about the Birth of the Savior*, by Jean-Daniel Kaestli), containing, at the very least, the journey to Bethlehem, the birth of Jesus, the story of the midwife, the visits of both the magi and shepherds, and perhaps some tales from the journey to Egypt. The combination of the works leads to some peculiar harmonizations—for example, the birth of Jesus in a cave according to the *Protevangelium* or in a stable according to *Pseudo-Matthew* are combined so that Jesus is born in a cave, then swaddled by Joseph [!], and placed in a manger. With respect to content, the description of the birth of Jesus is especially striking. As in the *Protevangelium*, there is a portrayal of nature standing still, though here from the perspective of the midwife rather than of Joseph. As in *Pseudo-Matthew*, there is mention of the brightly shining light that illuminates the cave during the event of the birth. While *Pseudo-Matthew* connects this with the splendor that is produced by the angels who are present at the birth, the *Book of the Savior* (chap. 73) connects it with the power of God that comes upon the child, who himself sends out rays like the sun (*solis modo*; a plausible correction of the text by James). Finally, it is said of this shining splendor that it fills the cave and even darkens the light of the sun. After this, it recedes into itself and takes the form of a child. This presentation of the birth of Jesus is sometimes characterized as "docetic"—i.e., as a description that suggests that Jesus only appeared (Greek *dokein* = appear) to be a human being. However, such a "heretical" view need not stand in the background. Rather, the work is concerned with emphasizing the divinity of Jesus, which could already be perceived at his birth. This tendency can be recognized in all the Infancy Gospels presented here. It surfaces especially clearly in the presentation of the birth of Jesus in the *Book of the Savior*.

The *Nativity of Mary* is a work that recounts the story of the parents of Mary, Joachim and Anna, the birth of Mary, her life in the sphere of the temple, the announcement of the birth of Jesus, the irritation of Joseph over Mary's pregnancy, and the birth of Jesus. It presupposes the *Protevangelium* and *Pseudo-Matthew* and presents itself as an expansion of the Gospels and ends with the trinitarian confession of "our Lord Jesus Christ who lives with the Father and the Holy Spirit and rules forever" (10:8; trans. Hawk). The work belongs to the Middle Ages and is attested for the first time in the eleventh century. It is a witness to the veneration of Mary, who is declared by the angel as a virgin who "will conceive without intercourse with a man, as a virgin . . . will give birth, as a virgin . . . will nurse" (9:9). Therefore, "the holy one born only of you, who alone is conceived without and born without sin, will be called the Son of God" (9:10, trans. Hawk).

The *History of Joseph the Carpenter* is often associated with the Infancy Gospels but it offers more than birth and childhood stories. The work was written for the veneration of Joseph, whose day of death is mentioned in the prologue. Different narrative features show that the conquering of death and the attaining of eternal life are important concerns of the text. The first part (1–11) is of interest for the childhood of Jesus.

The work is handed down in multiple Coptic and Arabic manuscripts. It was probably composed in Coptic in the sixth or seventh century. The Coptic textual witnesses suggest that the work was used in monastic circles in Egypt. It is introduced by a prologue that provides an introduction to the content and situation of emergence. It states that the Savior told the apostles the story of Joseph on the Mount of Olives and that the apostles wrote it down and preserved it in the library in Jerusalem, which is a common trope in Egyptian texts. After this, the story of Joseph is recounted as a report of Jesus about his father. Joseph begets four sons and two daughters with his wife. After the death of his wife, he takes Mary as his fiancée. The story of Mary includes the birth of Jesus, the flight to Egypt, and Jesus' childhood in the house of Joseph (7–11). A second part is devoted to the sickness and death of Joseph. The section features Joseph's prayer of lament as well as his last words to his son Jesus. These include an invocation of Jesus as Lord, King, Savior, and God, who is petitioned for support in distress and grief. Moreover, we find Joseph's cry of prayer: "You are Jesus Christ, the savior of my soul and my body and my spirit. Do not find fault with me, your servant and the work of your hands!" (17:7). In this prayer (17:10–14), Joseph also recalls episodes from Jesus' childhood, cobbled together by the author from several chapters of *Infancy Thomas* (4–5, 9, 16). Jesus departs from his narrative momentarily to exhort his disciples to remember his death on the cross for the life of the whole world and then resumes with a conversation with his mother, telling her she, like every human being, must die (18). After the presentation of the death and burial of Joseph, the framework story is taken up again (30–32). There is a dialogue between the apostles and Jesus about immortality and the fate of the dead.

The *Life of John the Baptist* is a homily for the dedication of a St. John's Church in Alexandria. There are at least ten manuscript witnesses of this text in Garšūnī—the Arabic language in Syriac script. The text was edited in 1927 based on two manuscripts from the sixteenth and eighteenth centuries. The editor, Alphonse Mingana, speculated that the text originated around the end of the fourth century CE in Greek. However, a recent study and new translation of the text by Slavomír Čéplö indicates that the Arabic text attested in the manuscripts took its form only much later, although earlier traditions may have been included. In the course of being handed down and translated it was then probably expanded and reworked. The present version shows clear signs of its use in monastic circles in Egypt. The first part is related to the childhood of Jesus. After that, John the Baptist moves more strongly into the foreground.

The text begins with an opening scene, in which the author—introduced simply as "we" but later identified as a bishop named Serapion—announces that he will write the life of John the Baptist, the son of Zechariah. After this, the announcements of the births of John the Baptist and Jesus, as well as the birth of John, the coming of the magi, and the massacre of the children are recounted. The narrative then follows John's life. He receives the mantle of Elijah and the belt of Elisha from the angel Gabriel. His mother flees with him into the wilderness, as in the *Protevangelium*. In chapter 5 the narrator turns directly to Elizabeth, who is praised for her rescuing of John, which took place at a time when there was neither a monastery nor a convent of monks. Elizabeth responds to the narrator that she did this "so that the mountains in the holy wilderness may become inhabited, and that communities of monks grow and multiply and offerings are made in them in the name of the Lord" (trans. Čéplö). In addition, the text recounts the death of Zechariah and Elizabeth as well as the visit of Jesus, Mary, and Salome to John, who they find alone in the wilderness, lamenting the death of his mother. After the burial of Elizabeth, whose day of death (February 15) is explicitly mentioned, John stays behind in the wilderness, whereas Mary and Jesus disappear again on the cloud that had brought them to John. This is followed by other episodes from the life of John that are known from the New Testament Gospels, including the baptism of Jesus and, finally, his beheading by Herod. His severed head, which can still see and speak, flies above the city for three years, and around the world for another fifteen, before coming to the ground in Homs (in Syria), where it is buried. His body is buried in Sebaste/Nablus in Samaria (13). From there the corpse, together with that of Elisha, is brought to Alexandria (14). At the end, the dedication of St. John's Church there is recounted.

Finally, reference may be made to Papyrus Cairensis 10735, a fragmentarily preserved papyrus page written on both sides, from among the papyrus cache discovered at Oxyrhynchus. It comes from the sixth or seventh century and was first published by the archeologists Grenfell and Hunt in 1903. The front side contains several lines of the narrative of the flight to Egypt and the back has the announcement of the birth of Jesus to Mary with a reference to the birth of John. This sequence is unique, but we do not know what work the text belonged to or what relation it has to the New Testament Gospels.

Conclusion

The Infancy Gospels display a clear interest in stories about Jesus' birth and childhood, his family, and the early life of John the Baptist. Starting from the stories of Matthew and Luke, they sketch out graphic, imaginative, and popular depictions of Jesus as a child, of the life of Mary and Joseph, and of the activity of the Baptist. These writings are not interested in the communication of historical knowledge but in the significance of Jesus and people in his environment for Christian piety and spirituality. Important concerns include the founding of Christian local traditions, the overcoming of existential challenges such as sickness and death, and the leading of a life in spiritual connection to the persons of the beginning period of Christianity. Connections to monastic life are often clearly recognizable. From early on, these writings have, therefore, played an important role for Christian piety and spirituality.

Sources and Studies

Aasgaard, Reidar. *The Childhood of Jesus: Decoding the Apocryphal Infancy Gospel of Thomas*. Eugene, OR: Cascade Books, 2009.

Budge, Ernest A. W., ed. and trans. *The History of the Blessed Virgin Mary and the History of the Likeness of Christ*. 2 vols. London: Luzac, 1899.

Burke, Tony, ed. and trans. *The Infancy Gospel of Thomas in the Syriac Tradition*. Gorgias Eastern Christian Studies 48. Piscataway, NJ: Gorgias, 2017.

———, ed. and trans. *De infantia Iesu euangelium Thomae graece*. CCSA 17. Turnhout: Brepols, 2010.

Čeplö, Slavomír, trans. "The Life of John the Baptist by Serapion." In *New Testament Apocrypha: More Noncanonical Scriptures*, vol. 1, edited by Tony Burke and Brent Landau, 268–92. Grand Rapids: Eerdmans, 2016.

Clivaz, Claire, et al., eds., *Infancy Gospels. Stories and Identities*. WUNT 281. Tübingen: Mohr/Siebeck, 2011.

Gijsel, Jan, and Rita Beyers, ed. and trans. *Libri de nativitate Mariae; textus et commentarius; Pseudo-Matthaei Evangelium; Libellus de nativitate Sanctae Mariae*. 2 vols. CCSA 9–10. Turnhout: Brepols, 1997.

Grenfell, Bernard P., and Arthur S. Hunt, eds. *Greek Papyri*. Oxford: Oxford University Press, 1903.

Hawk, Brandon W., ed. and trans. *The Gospel of Pseudo-Matthew and the Nativity of Mary*. Early Christian Apocrypha 8. Eugene, OR: Cascade Books, 2019.

Hock, Ronald F., ed. and trans. *The Infancy Gospels of James and Thomas*. The Scholars Bible 2. Santa Rosa, CA: Polebridge, 1995.

James, M. R., ed. *Latin Infancy Gospels: A New Text with a Parallel Version from Irish*. Cambridge: Cambridge University Press, 1927.

Kaestli, Jean-Daniel and Martin McNamara, eds. "Latin Infancy Gospels: The J Compilation, Introduction and Edition." In *Apocrypha Hiberniae I. Evangelia Infantiae*, edited by Martin McNamara et al., 2:621–880. 2 vols. CCSA 13–14. Turnhout: Brepols, 2001.

Mingana, Alphonse, ed. and trans. "A New Life of John the Baptist." In *Woodbrooke Studies: Christian Documents in Syriac, Arabic, and Garshuni*, vol. 1, edited by Alphonse Mingana, 138–45, 234–87. Cambridge: Cambridge University Press, 1927.

Postel, Guillaume. *Protevangelion, de seu de natalibus Iesu Christi et ipsius matris Virginis Mariae sermo historicus divi Iacobi Minoris*. Basel: Oporini, 1552

Provera, Mario E., ed. *Il Vangelo arabo dell'infanzia secondo il Ms. Laurenziano orientale (n. 387)*. Jerusalem: Franciscan Printing Press, 1973.

Schneider, Gerhard, ed. and trans. *Apokryphe Kindheitsevangelien*. New York: Herder, 1995.

Sike, Heinrich, ed. and trans. *Evangelium Infantiae; vel, Liber Apocryphus de Infantia Salvatoris; ex manuscripto edidit, ac Latina versione et notis illustravit Henricus Sike*. Utrecht: Halman, 1697.

Strycker, Émile de. *La forme la plus ancienne du Protévangile de Jacques*. Subsidia Hagiographica 33. Brussels: Société des Bollandistes, 1961.

Terian, Abraham, ed. and trans. *The Armenian Gospel of the Infancy with Three Early Versions of the Protevangelium of James*. Oxford: Oxford University Press, 2008.

Vuong, Lily C., trans. *The Protevangelium of James*. Early Christian Apocrypha 7. Eugene, OR: Cascade Books, 2019.

Wayment, Thomas, and Alexander Ladenheim. "A New Fragment of the *Protevangelium Jacobi*." HTR 104 (2011) 381–84.

3

Traditions about the Ministry of Jesus

Introduction

DIVERSE TRADITIONS ABOUT THE ministry of Jesus can be found outside the New Testament. These are extant in fragmentarily preserved texts or texts handed down only in quotations; there are no known extra-canonical gospels that contain a complete narrative of the activity of Jesus. This does not mean that such narratives did not exist. But the content and literary shape of the writings to which the extant fragments belonged can no longer be reconstructed. The relevant fragments will be discussed, therefore, with a view to the interpretations of the activity of Jesus that are recognizable in them.

The "Jewish-Christian" Gospels

Writings that engage with Jesus from a perspective in which Jewish traditions play an important role are designated by modern scholars as Jewish-Christian Gospels. This is misleading insofar as other gospels also develop a clearly Jewish view of Jesus—for example, the Gospels of Matthew and Luke as well as the *Protevangelium*. Indeed, quite a few other writings of early Christianity share this Jewish view of Jesus. Moreover, the term "Jewish-Christian" was only introduced in the modern period for the purpose of distinguishing directions of thought based on Judaism from those that draw on non-Jewish traditions. The term "Jewish-Christian" could also be combined with the view that Christianity comes to itself only when it leaves Judaism behind. Today, this extremely problematic view has hardly any advocates in Christian theology.

The designation is also problematic insofar as it suggests a distinction between Jewish-Christian Gospels and gospels that are not based on Jewish traditions, though the conditions were much more complex. Jewish traditions lived on in many streams of Christianity and their writings, so that it is scarcely possible to draw a clear line of division between "Jewish" and "Christian." Thus, there never was a sharply contoured "Jewish-Christianity." Nevertheless, groups are attested that believed in Jesus Christ and oriented themselves to Jewish rituals—i.e., they continued to circumcise male children, kept the Sabbath, and observed the dietary restrictions. The Jewish-Christian Gospels are also connected with such groups.

These gospels are attested only in the writings of early Christian theologians; we do not possess a single manuscript of such a gospel. The statements about the relevant groups and writings in the works of ancient authors do not present a clear picture. This is partly due to the fact that the relevant notes do not agree with one another, and the assignments of writings to certain groups are not always clear. The situation is also complicated by the fact that according to Papias, a bishop in Asia Minor in the second century CE, the Gospel of Matthew was originally written in Hebrew, a statement that is sometimes brought into connection with the Jewish-Christian Gospels:

> Matthew then in Hebrew language compiled the oracles, and each person translated them as each was able. (quoted in Eusebius, *Hist. eccl.* 3.39.16)

The question of how many Jewish-Christian Gospels existed is controversial due to the non-uniform information of early Christian theologians who sometimes refer to one work with two designations or say that a gospel was used by a certain group. After a long time in which modern scholars predominately held the view that there was only one such gospel (namely, the *Gospel according to the Hebrews*), the view that there must have been at least two and possibly even three (or even more) of these writings has now come to the fore. Final certainty cannot, however, be achieved here.

The Apocryphal Gospels

The *Gospel according to the Hebrews*

The only Jewish-Christian Gospel attested by name is the *Gospel according to the Hebrews*. The earliest mention of it occurs at the end of the second century CE in Clement of Alexandria's work *Miscellanies*. Clement quotes a saying there, which he introduces with the statement "As it is also written in the Gospel according to the Hebrews: "The one who is amazed will rule, and the one who rules will find rest" (*Strom.* 2.9.45). This saying occurs again a bit later (5.96.3) in a more detailed version. In this text there is talk of seeking and finding that leads to rule and to rest. A similar version is also attested in the *Gospel of Thomas* (saying 2). Only in the first case is the saying traced back explicitly to *Hebrews*. It is no longer possible to say what the context of the saying was in the original text. Clement quotes it in the context of remarks on amazement as the beginning of philosophy and mentions Plato as the first witness for this.

Another reference to *Hebrews* occurs a little later in time in Origen's commentary on the Gospel of John. He introduces a quotation there with "If anyone accepts the Gospel according to the Hebrews . . ." and then quotes a saying of the "Savior": "Just now my mother, the Holy Spirit, took me by one of my hairs and carried me up to the great mountain, Tabor" (*Comm. Jo.* 2.12). The saying appears again in Origen's homilies on the book of Jeremiah 15:4 (without mention of its source). In his commentaries on the books of Micah (7:4), Isaiah (11:1–3), and Ezekiel (18:7), Jerome quotes a saying of the Savior (or the Lord) who says "my mother, the Holy Spirit led (took, raptured) me," each time with a specification of *Hebrews* as the source. Apparently, then, *Hebrews* contained a variant of the story of the temptation of Jesus, where both the Spirit and (in Matthew and Luke) a mountain play a role. In *Hebrews*, Jesus himself gives an account of his temptation, with him designating the Holy Spirit as his mother, which apparently offends Origen, since "Spirit" is not feminine in Greek—it is, however, feminine in Hebrew, which could stand in the background of the tradition. In his commentary on Micah, Jerome also notes that he recently translated *Hebrews*; in the two other passages he says that *Hebrews* was read by the "Nazarenes."

In addition, an episode is handed down in Jerome that he says he translated into Greek and Latin from the gospel named "according to the Hebrews," which Origen is also said to have often used (*Vir. ill.* 2). According to it, Jesus appeared to James (his brother) after the resurrection, and after that, he celebrated the meal with him. The episode contains echoes of other known resurrection traditions (especially of the linen cloth mentioned in John 20:5–7), of the appearance of Jesus to James (1 Cor 15:7, as well as the *Apocryphon of James*; see also saying 13 of the *Gospel of Thomas*), and of the meals of the Risen One (Luke 24:30; John 21:13; Acts 1:4). This connection can be clearly recognized in the expression "He took the bread and blessed it, broke it, gave it to James ..." Jerome also mentions a variant of the narrative of the baptism of Jesus:

> It is stated in the Gospel written in Hebrew, which the Nazareans read: "The entire fountain of the Holy Spirit will descend on him. And the Lord is Spirit, and where the Spirit of the Lord is, there is liberty." Later in that Gospel that we have mentioned above we find the following written: "Then, when the Lord came up from the water, the entire fountain of the Holy Spirit descended and rested on him; and it said to him, "My Son, in all the prophets I have been expecting you to come, that I might rest on you. For you are my rest, you are my firstborn Son, who rules forever." (*Comm. Isa.* 11.1–3)

Beyond this, *Hebrews* apparently contained an exhortation to brotherly love, the episode about the encounter of Jesus with a sinful woman, and a note about the identification of the Matthias selected to replace Judas (Acts 1:15–26) with the Levi called by Jesus, who is called Matthew in the Gospel of Matthew (Matthew 9:9//Luke 5:27):

> And in the Gospel according to the Hebrews, which the Nazareans are accustomed to read, the following is among the worst offenses: that someone should make the spirit of his brother sad. (Jerome, *Comm. Ezech.* 18.7)
>
> It seems that Matthew is named Levi in the Gospel of Luke. But this is not he; it is Matthias, the one who replaced Judas, who is the same as Levi, known by two names. This appears in the Gospel according to the Hebrews. (Didymus the Blind, *Comm. Ps.* 184.9–10)

For other fragments, the assignment remains uncertain. In particular, the distinction between the *Gospel according to the Hebrews* and a "Gospel of the Nazareans" is not clear. It is not possible to say with ultimate certainty whether there was, in fact, a "Gospel of the Nazareans" or whether, alternatively, the relevant statements of Jerome are to be related to *Hebrews*. In the latter case, our knowledge of *Hebrews* would be expanded further. The following remarks shall make this ambiguity clear.

The *Gospel of the Nazareans*

In the Latin revision of Origen's *Commentary on Matthew* (15.14; not in the Greek original) there is a parallel to Jesus' dialogue on the obtaining of eternal life from the New Testament Gospels. The episode is introduced with the words "It is written in a certain Gospel that is called 'according to the Hebrews'" and followed by the note that this gospel enjoys no authority but can serve as confirmation for the question that is under discussion at this point in the commentary. The following episode displays some differences from Matthew 19:16–24 and the parallels in Mark and Luke. Apparently, the Latin editor has subsequently expanded this piece with knowledge of the Synoptic Gospels. In that case, it would not come from the "Gospel according to the Hebrews" known to Origen but from the *Gospel of the Nazareans*.

Another episode is found in Eusebius (*Theophania* 4.22). He quotes an ethicizing interpretation of the parable of the talents (Matthew 25:14–30) from a "Gospel that has come down to us in Hebrew letters." The phrase "in Hebrew letters" could refer to the Aramaic linguistic form of the gospel. Since *Hebrews* is quoted by the Alexandrian, Greek-speaking theologians Clement and Origen, it was probably written in Greek. The designation "according to the Hebrews" does not speak against this, for it refers not to the language but to the origin of the writing from Jewish-Christians. In that case, *Nazareans* would need to be distinguished from it. However, Jerome's statement that he translated *Hebrews* into Greek and Latin would then need to be regarded as inaccurate.

Other fragments appear in Jerome. He twice refers to the translation of a word in the Lord's Prayer, which is difficult in Greek, because it is not attested elsewhere, namely the word "daily" in the expression "daily bread":

> In the Hebrew Gospel according to Matthew it says this: 'Our bread for tomorrow give us today,' this means: 'The bread, that you will give us in your kingdom, give us today.' (*Comm. Ps.* 135; trans. Elliot)
>
> In the Gospel that is called "according to the Hebrews," for the words, "bread to sustain our lives" I found the word "Mahar," which means "[bread] for tomorrow." (*Comm. Matt.* 6.11)

In the same commentary, Jerome refers to a work that he designates as the "Gospel that the Nazarenes and the Ebionites use, which I recently translated from Hebrew into Greek and which most people consider the authentic version of Matthew" (*Comm. Matt.* 12.13). He also mentions a "Gospel according to the Hebrews, which was actually written in the Chaldean or Syriac language but with Hebrew letters, which the Nazareans use still today and which is that according to the Apostles, or, as most believe, according to Matthew" (*Pelag.* 3.2). He quotes various episodes and information from this work, which sometimes possess analogies to the New Testament Gospels—for example, an episode on the baptism of Jesus (*Pelag.* 3.2), a variant of the healing of the man with the withered hand on the Sabbath (*Comm. Matt.* 12.13; which is explicitly set in relation to the Gospel of Matthew), and the dialogue between Jesus and Simon (Peter) about the readiness to forgive (*Pelag.* 3.2)—but sometimes also involve linguistic variants or an interpretation of a name (Barabbas is interpreted as "son of a teacher," *Comm. Matt.* 27.51). Medieval witnesses assign some other material to a "Gospel of the Nazoreans" or to a Gospel "according to the Hebrews."

These findings can best be explained as follows: in addition to the Greek *Gospel according to the Hebrews*, there was an *Aramaic Gospel of the Nazareans*. The note about the use of the latter by the Nazarenes or Ebionites is, however, as uncertain as the note about a connection with a supposedly original Hebrew Gospel of Matthew. It seems that Jerome is attempting to combine various pieces of information, without precise knowledge of the relevant texts and groups.

While these two writings apparently contained episodes and sayings of Jesus that are related to the New Testament Gospels, nothing exact can be determined about their scope and literary form. In the case of *Hebrews*, we could be dealing with a gospel from the Alexandrian milieu that displays points of contact with Jewish wisdom theology: Wisdom is the mother of Jesus, the saying about seeking and finding has philosophical analogies, and the encounter of the Risen One with James accentuates the significance of the resurrection and post-Easter appearance of Jesus from a Jewish-Christian perspective—and thus in a rather different way than the Dialogue Gospels that we will discuss later (Part 5). By contrast, *Nazareans* appears to have possessed a closer affinity to the Gospel of Matthew. It apparently had an Aramaic origin. It focusses on ethical concerns with its emphasis on the observance of the law and prophets and with its interpretation of the parable of the talents. The episode about the healing of Jesus on the Sabbath explains why the man wishes to be healed. He is a mason and needs to earn his livelihood. This serves to remove the offensiveness of the healing on the Sabbath. The fragments thus point to different milieus of language and tradition, thereby suggesting a division into two different writings.

The *Gospel of the Ebionites*

Only in Epiphanius of Salamis do we find a few quotations that he assigns to one of the writings used by the "Ebionites." Epiphanius was a bishop on Cyprus who composed a large work against all the heresies known to him with the title *Panarion* or *Medicine Chest*. In most cases he knew the groups that he describes only through hearsay, which probably also applies to the "Ebionites." The concern is with a Jewish-Christian group who apparently lived in the land east of the Jordan. Irenaeus mentions that they used the Gospel of Matthew. Epiphanius also says that the gospel used by the Ebionites was called "according to Matthew" or, alternatively the "Hebrew Gospel." The work that is quoted by Epiphanius could, therefore, represent a revised version of the Gospel of Matthew into which traditions from other Synoptic Gospels have flowed. The name "Gospel of the Ebionites," however, is neither attested by manuscripts nor mentioned by ancient authors. Rather, it was first assigned to the work in modern scholarship.

According to Epiphanius, the work began with the baptism of Jesus by John "in the days of Herod, King of Judea," whereas the preceding genealogy of Jesus was removed (*Pan.* 30.13.6; 30.14.3). Thus, the *Gospel of the Ebionites* had no interest in the virgin birth. It could fit with this that the baptism of Jesus is interpreted with the scriptural saying "Today I have begotten you" (*Pan.* 30.13.3–4), which is lacking in the New Testament Gospels (with the exception of a few manuscripts of the Gospel of Luke). The baptism is thus interpreted as a transformation of Jesus into the Son of God through the union with the divine Spirit.

It is recounted further that Jesus, at the age of about thirty years, "chose us." This is followed by a list of eight names of disciples, which is presented as the direct speech of Jesus and is addressed at the end to "Matthew, you who sat at the toll booth." At the end it says, "I want you, therefore, to be the twelve apostles as a witness to Israel" (*Pan.* 30.13.2–3). This fragment is distinctive in the fact that it is told from the perspective of the apostles. For this reason, the suggestion has sometimes been made that it should be assigned to another writing—perhaps a "Gospel of the Twelve Apostles," which is mentioned by Origen (*Hom. Luc.* 1.1–2; see the quotation in chap. 1 above) and after him by Jerome, and others. This remains unclear, however, especially since nothing else is known about that work.

Finally, we encounter the episode about the "true relatives" of Jesus, which also appears in the Synoptics. It declares those to be his family "who do the will of my Father" (*Pan.* 30.14.5). According to Epiphanius, the Ebionites, through an appeal to this text, deny that Jesus is a human being, since he would reject having earthly, bodily relatives. This interpretation can be reconciled only with difficulty with the otherwise recognizable tendencies of the *Gospel of the Ebionites* and may go back to a misinterpretation by Epiphanius.

It may be possible to recognize in *Ebionites* the intention of distinguishing more clearly between the divine and the human nature of Jesus than was the case in the Christian teaching that was becoming established. However, we must take into account the fact that Epiphanius has selected the quotations in such a way that the characteristics of the Ebionites that he criticizes emerge clearly. Moreover, we must consider that with respect to one of the most difficult christological questions—the relationship between the divine and human nature of Jesus Christ—there was, from the earliest period, a broad spectrum of positions, which is now only discernible through the perspective of the Christian theologians who ultimately held sway as an opposition between "orthodox" and "heretical" positions. In this question, the Ebionites could have advocated a view of Jesus as a human being who came from Judaism and became Son of God through the union with the divine Spirit, a position that was ultimately incompatible with the christological creed of the early church.

The *Gospel according to the Egyptians*

A "Gospel according to the Egyptians" is mentioned by Clement, Origen, Hippolytus, and Epiphanius. Origen mentions it among the rejected gospels, and Clement explicitly distinguishes it from the "four Gospels handed down to us."

> Those who oppose God's creation through self-control—which sounds good—also quote the words spoken to Salome, some of which we have already mentioned, found, I think, in the Gospel according to the Egyptians. For they claim that the Savior himself said, "I have come to destroy the works of the female." By

> "the female" he meant desire and by "works" he meant birth and degeneration. (Clement of Alexandria, *Strom.* 3.63.1)
>
> This is why Cassian says, "When Salome inquired when the things she had asked about would become known, the Lord replied: 'When you (pl.) trample on the garment of shame and when the two become one and the male with the female is neither male nor female.'" The first thing to note, then, is that we do not find this saying in the four Gospels handed down to us, but in the Gospel according to the Egyptians. (Clement of Alexandria, *Strom.* 3.92.2–93.1)

Origen mentions a "Gospel according to the Egyptians" among the rejected gospels of the heretics in his Homilies on the Gospel of Luke (see the quotation above in the introduction). According to Hippolytus the gnostic group of the Naasenes used *Egyptians* for their specific teaching about the soul (*Haer.* 5.7.2–9). Epiphanius mentions them among diverse heretical Christian groups (*Pan.* 62.2.4). Quotations from *Egyptians* occur only in Clement's works. Thus, the work must have arisen in the second century. These quotations seem to be taken from a dialogue between Jesus and Salome, from which it can perhaps be inferred that the writing as a whole was a dialogue. Thus, some more quotations from Clement containing a dialogue between Jesus ("the Lord") and Salome are often regarded as coming from *Egyptians* as well:

> When Salome asked, "How long will death prevail?" the Lord replied, "For as long as you women bear children." But he did not say this because life is evil or the creation wicked; instead he was teaching the natural succession of things; for everything degenerates after coming into being. (*Strom.* 3.45.3)
>
> Therefore it is probably with regard to the final consummation, as the argument indicates, that Salome says, "How long will people continue to die?" Now Scripture refers to a human being in two senses: that which is visible and the soul, that is, one subject to salvation and one not. And sin is called the death of the soul. For this reason, the Lord also replied shrewdly, "For as long as women bear children"—that is to say, for as long as desires continue to be active. (*Strom.* 3.64.1)
>
> Why do those who adhere more to everything other than the true gospel rule not cite the following words spoken to Salome? For when she said, "Then I have done well not to bear children" (supposing that it was not necessary to give birth), the Lord responded, "Eat every herb, but not the one that is bitter." (*Strom.* 3.66.1–2)

> And when the Savior said to Salome, "Death will last as long as women give birth," he was not denigrating birth—since it is, after all, necessary for the salvation of those who believe. (*Exc.* 67.2)

If these passages belonged to the same writing, namely from a "Gospel according to the Egyptians," it could be inferred that this writing had the form of a dialogue between Jesus (perhaps the Risen One) and Salome who is mentioned in the Gospel of Mark among the women who were looking from a distance at Jesus' crucifixion (15:40) and who went to his tomb on Easter morning (16:1). In this case, *Egyptians* could have been a Dialogue Gospel, such as the *Gospel of Mary* and the *Wisdom of Jesus Christ*, which will be discussed later.

Occasionally, additional quotations from other writings were regarded as part of *Egyptians*. In particular, the following quotation from *2 Clement*, a homily from the middle of the second century, is adduced in this regard:

> For the Lord himself, when he was asked by someone when his kingdom was going to come, said: "When the two shall be one, and the outside like the inside, and the male with the female, neither male nor female." (*2 Clem.* 12.2; trans. Holmes)

The fragment deals with the idea of an original unity of male and female which also occurs in the two passages of Clement of Alexandria that quote *Egyptians*. However, it cannot be stated with certainty that *2 Clement* 12.2 indeed belonged to *Egyptians* or whether it is just a noncanonical saying of Jesus (*agraphon*) which occurs in different contexts. Therefore, the assumption of previous research that also other Jesus sayings in *2 Clement* derive from *Egyptians* cannot be sustained.

The quotations in Clement of Alexandria suggest that *Egyptians* was especially concerned with sexual asceticism (this impression could, however, also be a result of the selection of the quotations by Clement). Thus, Jesus answers Salome's question about the length of time that death will have power with "For as long as you women bear children" (*Strom.* 3.45.3; 3.64.1; *Exc.* 67.2). As explicitly noted, this is not meant to designate life or creation as evil but to refer to the natural sequence of emergence and decay. The next quotation also points in this direction. According to it, the Savior said "I have come to destroy the works of the female" (*Strom.* 3.63.1). This saying, which is quoted by those who, according to Clement, oppose the order of God through sexual abstinence, shows the same tendency that is also recognizable in the *Dialogue of the Savior* and the *Gospel of Thomas* (on these texts, see the relevant sections below), and it also occurs in *2 Clement*—namely, the annulment of the division of the sexes as a presupposition for salvation through the dissolution of the female. Clement weakens the saying by explaining that by "the female," Jesus meant desire. This tendency can also be recognized in another quotation: "When you trample on the garment of shame and when the two become one and the male with the female is neither male nor female" (*Strom.* 3.92.2–93.1). Here too, Clement interprets the saying in a figurative sense: by "the male impulse" Jesus meant anger and by the female impulse he meant desire.

Thus, in the *Gospel according to the Egyptians*, the theme of salvation through sexual abstinence and overcoming the distinction between the sexes appears to play an important role. This was developed in the form of a conversation between Jesus and Salome. It is no longer possible to say what scope and literary character the writing as a whole had.

Papyrus Egerton 2 (and Papyrus Köln 255)

Papyrus Egerton 2 consists of four papyrus pages written on both sides that belonged to a codex. The name comes from the patron who enabled the British Museum to purchase it in 1934. The first edition, by H. I. Bell and T. C. Skeat, appeared the following year. The fragments can be dated to the second half of the second century CE, placing them among the oldest preserved Christian manuscripts. There is identifiable text only on two of the pages. Fragment 1 could also be expanded by a few lines at the lower margin through a fragment in the Cologne papyrus collection (P.Köln 255) that belongs to the same codex. The third fragment contains a few letters and the fourth only a single letter. Fragment 3 may have contained a version of the saying "I and the Father are one" (cf. John 10:30), followed by the decision to kill Jesus. The remains of the letters "one are (we)" as well as "ki(l)" could point to this. On the other pages there are quite a few linguistic and content commonalities with the Gospel of John. But the few legible letters do not allow for more than a vague supposition.

Some terms are written as *nomina sacra* ("holy names") on the pages. This is a system of writing in which certain words are abbreviated, usually through two or three letters, and signaled by a horizontal line over them. The words in question are usually important names and terms, especially

"God," "Jesus," "Lord," "Christ," and "Spirit." This system is found only in Christian manuscripts, and from a very early time onward. They usually occur in manuscripts of biblical texts. P.Egerton 2 shows, however, that *nomina sacra* also occasionally appear in non-biblical texts. P.Egerton 2 is an early example for this. It is notable that in addition to "God," "Jesus," and "Lord," the scribe of P.Egerton 2 also wrote some designations as *nomina sacra* that do not appear in this form in biblical texts. These include "Moses," "Isaiah," "prophets," "prophesy," and "king." This unusual use of *nomina sacra* may indicate that in the relatively early time in which the text was written, the system had not yet been developed in the way that it is developed in later manuscripts.

On the two pages with legible text, the papyrus contains episodes from the activity of Jesus. Thereby, connections to the Synoptic Gospels can be observed, especially in an episode about the healing of a leper (Mark 1:40–44 and par.) and in the question of whether the disciples of Jesus should pay taxes (Mark 12:13–17 and par.). However, there are also linguistic and content-related connections to the Gospel of John—for example, in the statement that "the hour of the handing over" of Jesus has not yet come (7:30, 44), in the exhortation to search the Scriptures (5:39), in the reference to the fact that the Scriptures bear witness to Jesus (5:45–46), and in the phrase "and sin no more" (5:14; 8:11) as the conclusion of the story of the healing of the leper.

Since the manuscript fragments lack page numbers, the original sequence of the material remains hypothetical. It can be postulated, however, that we are dealing with a writing after the manner of the New Testament Gospels, in which incidents from the life of Jesus were narrated in a continuous manner.

Fragment 1, verso, contains a dispute of Jesus with the "teachers of the law" and "rulers of the people" over the meaning of the Scriptures. Jesus says to them that the Scriptures testify concerning him and that Moses, in whom they have placed their hope, accuses them. They respond that they know that God has spoken to Moses but do not know where he (Jesus) is from. Jesus answers with an accusation of their unbelief, because they have not recognized that Moses wrote about him (Jesus).

The other side of the page (recto) begins with the fragmentarily preserved statement that they (according to the incomplete first line, the crowd is apparently in view) gather stones to stone him. As a second group, the "rulers" then appear (the leaders of the people are in view, though only a few letters of this word are preserved) who seize Jesus and seek to hand him over (?) to the crowd. This is followed by the expression, reminiscent of the Gospel of John, "But they were not able to arrest him, for the hour for him to be handed over had not yet come" (cf. John 7:30; 8:20; 10:39). Jesus passes through their midst and distances himself from them. Both episodes point to the conflict between Jesus and the Jewish crowd as well as its leaders as an important theme.

The episode that immediately follows recounts Jesus' encounter with a leper. An analogy to this occurs in Mark 1:40-44 and in the parallels in Matthew 8:1-4 and Luke 5:12-16. The distinctive feature in comparison to the Synoptic versions is the fact that the leper traces back his sickness to the fact that he traveled with lepers with whom he ate and thereby became unclean himself. The petition for the restoration of purity is fulfilled by Jesus, who is addressed here as "teacher," through the words "I wish, become clean." There follows the instruction of Jesus to the healed person to show himself to the priest and present the purification offering prescribed by Moses, which is mainly preserved in the Cologne papyrus.

The specific feature of the narrative lies in the leper's explanation regarding the origin of his sickness or impurity. It is apparently a consequence of his transgression of the purity commandments that prohibit Jews from coming into contact with what is impure—i.e., also with impure people. To this corresponds Jesus' concluding exhortation to the healed person to present the purification offering prescribed by Moses. Perhaps we should also assign to this the narrative feature that Jesus—in contrast to what we find in the Synoptic Gospels—does not touch the leper in the healing, perhaps in order not to defile himself. Finally, the expression "and sin no more" at the end of the episode—which is also Johannine—speaks for this interpretation. The formulation also occurs in John 5:14 as well as in the episode about Jesus' encounter with an adulteress (John 7:53-8:11), which was added to the Gospel of John after its composition. Thus, the impurity of the leper is interpreted in P.Egerton 2 as a consequence of his transgression of the Jewish law. Accordingly, the episode can be best understood as another variant of the healing story. A direct dependence on the Synoptic Gospels, however, is not recognizable.

Fragment 2, verso, contains text that is preserved only in very fragmentary form. It is possible—as the recently proposed reconstruction by Lorne Zelyck has it—that the second part, from line 6, contains the story of a miracle that Jesus performed at the Jordan. It is recognizable that Jesus comes to the shore of the Jordan, extends his hand, and sows something, presumably on the river. It could be an analogy to the miracle that is recounted about Elisha in 2 Kings 2:19–22. The text's Elisha typology could also be reinforced by the fact that an exact linguistic parallel to the expression "and he stood on the shore of the Jordan" occurs in the Greek text of 2 Kings 2:13 and only there. In the miracle that is recounted a little later in 2 Kings 2, Elisha transforms bad water into healthy water. The narrative of this miracle in the work of the Jewish historian Josephus (*Jewish War* 4.460–464) can help to reconstruct the fragmentary text on P.Egerton 2. Thus, this could have recounted that Jesus sowed salt in the water of the Jordan and that this bore fruit in (or on?) the water. Even though many details remain hypothetical due to the poorly preserved text, the hypothesis can be advanced that Fragment 2 recounts a miracle of Jesus dependent upon the Elisha tradition, perhaps in analogy to the motif of the bearing of fruit in the Synoptic parables of sowing (cf., for example, Mark 4:2–9).

Fragment 2, recto, contains, once again, a conflict scene. At the beginning, the phrase "they tested him" is preserved, followed by the address "we know that you have come [from God]. For the things you do give a testimony that is beyond all the prophets." This is followed by the question of whether it is right to pay kings what is due to their regime. Jesus recognizes the intention of his enemies to trap him, becomes angry, and answers with a saying of the prophet Isaiah: "This people honors me with their lips, but their heart is far removed from me. In vain do they worship me" (29:13).

The episodes preserved on P.Egerton 2 point to a Jesus narrative in which the conflict between Jesus and the Jewish authorities as well as with the Jewish people plays an important role. The controversial themes here are the authority to interpret the Scriptures of Israel and the observance of the Jewish law. Jesus claims authority in relation to both and simultaneously denies them to his opponents. Jesus is addressed as "teacher" by the protagonists of the narrative, whereas he is designated as "Lord" or with his name "Jesus" by the narrator. He possesses the authority to perform miracles and knows himself to be in an exclusive relationship with God, his Father.

P.Egerton 2 evidently recounts the story of Jesus in a distinctive way that differs from the New Testament Gospels, even though linguistic and content-related connections are recognizable. This shows that at an early period in time more narratives of Jesus than the four Gospels that made it into the New Testament already existed. It is no longer possible to determine, however, what form and content-related features the text, to which P.Egerton 2 belonged, exhibited.

Papyrus Oxyrhynchus 840

Only a single page is preserved of Papyrus Oxyrhynchus 840 (P.Oxy. 840). It was discovered in 1905 and first published, again by Grenfell and Hunt, in 1908. Although it is designated a "papyrus," it is actually a parchment page. It has the astonishingly small size of 8.6 × 7.2 cm, with the space that is written on being 5.5 × 5.2 cm. On this, there are 45 lines of text (!), with 22 on the hair side and 23 on the flesh side. The size of the codex led to the hypothesis that it could be an amulet that was worn for protection against evil powers, demons, or sicknesses. This practice was widespread in antiquity, including in Judaism and Christianity. Magical formulas could be found on amulets, and yet also biblical texts, such as Psalms, the Lord's Prayer, and other texts from the Gospels.

P.Oxy. 840 belonged, however, to a very small codex—a "miniature codex." It was not a single page that could have served as an amulet. How exactly to specify the relationship between amulets and miniature codices is a topic of discussion in contemporary scholarship. It is plausible that very small codices could *also* have served as items that could be carried around. Moreover, it must be considered that the extremely small writing on a codex such as the one to which P.Oxy. 840 belonged can be read only with difficulty. On the other hand, the codex format indicates that the text did not serve merely apotropaic—i.e., disaster averting—purposes, but was also meant to pass on Jesus traditions. It is possible that there were mixed forms between amulets and miniature codices, so that the two need not stand in strict opposition to each other.

The codex has been dated to the first half of the fourth century, but the text itself could come from the second century CE. In some places, words are written as *nomina sacra*—in lines 5 and 39 for "human beings," in lines 12, 21, and 30 for "Savior," and in line 25 for "David." The scribe has placed special stress on a letter (by writing it larger) in lines 7, 30, and 41, apparently in order to mark the beginning of a new section. Moreover, red ink is used for dots, supralinear lines, and accents. In three places, words or parts of words that were apparently omitted when it was written have been subsequently added. It is noteworthy that a non-biblical text was produced with such an elaborate form in a fourth century text.

TRADITIONS ABOUT THE MINISTRY OF JESUS

The extant text contains the end of a speech of Jesus and an episode attached to it. The speech ends with a warning—apparently to the disciples of Jesus—to guard themselves against becoming like evildoers, because they must suffer punishment and great torture. After this, Jesus goes with his disciples into the temple area—the episode thus takes place in Jerusalem—where they meet a Pharisee and chief priest whose name is presumably Levi (this is, however, uncertain due to the poorly preserved end of the line). He accuses Jesus of defiling "this holy place," since neither he nor his disciples are washed, and they had not changed their clothing. Levi, by contrast, has washed in the "pool of David," has gone down by one set of steps and come up by another, and has put on white clothes before he looked at the "holy vessels."

Jesus, who is always called "Savior" in the text, responds with a sharp criticism that characterizes the purity of the Pharisees as a purely external purity to which no inner purity corresponds. He and his disciples, in contrast, had bathed in "living waters that come from above."

There are several notable features of the text. First, the Greek term *hagneutērion* for "temple area" (or "purity area") is never used elsewhere in Jewish and early Christian texts and is attested only three other times in Greek literature as a whole (once in the work of a Stoic from the first century, twice in the Christian theologian Gregory of Nazianzus in the fourth century). The designation "pool of David" is also not attested elsewhere. The characterization of the opponent of Jesus as "Pharisee" and "chief priest" is also conspicuous. To be sure, there are occasional attestations for Pharisees being "chief priests" (or high priests), but this happened only very rarely. Instead, we get the impression that two traits that characterize the relevant person as an opponent of Jesus are being united here—his insistence on the purity commandments and his function at the Jerusalem temple.

The linguistic shaping of the text lets the focus on the theme of "purity" emerge clearly. In addition to the terminology mentioned above, we find the terms "sanctuary," "holy vessels," "holy place," "pure," "wash," and, as an opposing term, "defile." Moreover, some terms are more reminiscent of the Christian ritual of baptism than the Jewish rites of purification: "immerse," "go down by one set of steps, come up by another," "white and pure clothes," as well as the mention of flowing water.

Furthermore, it must be asked whether the author possessed accurate historical information about Judaism at the time of Jesus and its rites of purification. This question has been controversial since the beginning of the discussion of the fragment, and it remains so. Here, there is disagreement between, on the one hand, those who argue that the fragment displays reliable knowledge about Jerusalem, the temple, and Jewish traditions and thus belongs in the context of Jesus or of the early conflict between Judaism and Christianity and, on the other hand, those who point to specifications that are imprecise or inaccurate and have echoes of baptism and, therefore, the text must be of later origin. If we consider the controversy presented in the fragment between an opponent of Jesus, who is oriented to purity through washing, and Jesus' own position, which is oriented to the purity through "living water that comes from above," then more speaks for the view that a dispute between two Christian strands and their respective views of baptism is reflected here. The one strand, which is oriented to water baptism, is represented by the Pharisee and chief priest Levi, whereas Jesus advocates a spiritual baptism, as a ritual that forges a connection with the sphere above. According to this interpretation, P.Oxy. 840 would be a specific reception and continuation of disputes over purity between Jesus and the Pharisees that is now placed in the context of an inner-Christian controversy over baptism, which is understood either as water baptism or as "spiritual baptism," which does not require earthly water. Such controversies point to the second and third centuries CE, when the view of a direct approach to the heavenly sphere that does not require water baptism was advocated, for example, by gnostic groups, whereas it was rejected by Christian theologians such as Irenaeus and Hippolytus. The narrative in P.Oxy. 840 could belong in such a context. However, the overarching literary form and content of the codex to which the episode belonged must remain an open question.

Additional Fragments

In addition to the aforementioned texts, episodes from the activity of Jesus are attested by a few other fragments. Papyrus Merton 51 is a small papyrus page written on both sides that is only 3.9 × 5.3 cm in size. It dates from the third century. The name comes from the collector Wilfred Merton, who died in 1917 and to whose collection the papyrus belonged. It was first published in 1959 by B. R. Rees. In the manuscript, the Greek term for "God" (*theos*) is written twice—or possibly three times—as a *nomen sacrum* (recto, lines 2, 5, and possibly 6). The papyrus is severely damaged on one side, so that quite a bit must be supplemented. From the preserved remains, two episodes can be reconstructed that display a close connection to the Gospel of Luke. On the recto, a relationship to Luke 7:29–30 can be discerned: The people and the Pharisees acknowledge God to be just and confess their sins, whereas the Pharisees do not let themselves be baptized by John and reject the counsel of God. This is followed by the beginning of an episode in which a Pharisee invites Jesus to eat (cf. Luke 7:36). On the verso, there is a variant to Luke 6:45–46, the saying about the bad person who brings forth what is bad, as a bad tree bears bad fruit, followed by the exhortation not only to call Jesus "Lord, Lord," but also to do what he says. The papyrus could be a homily or commentary on the Gospel of Luke. It is also conceivable, however, that it belonged to a gospel that is not otherwise known, which had points of contact—at least in the preserved passages—to the Gospel of Luke.

Papyrus Oxyrhynchus 1224 consists of two fragments, with a large amount of text being preserved only on the second of these. The papyrus was published in 1914 and dates from the fourth century CE. The editors Grenfell and Hunt assigned it, together with three other papyri that contain sayings of Jesus or shorter episodes (P.Oxy. 1, 654, and 655), to an unknown gospel. Since then, the latter three papyri have been judged to be Greek remnants of the *Gospel of Thomas* (on this, see the discussion in chap. 5 below). On the fragments of P.Oxy. 1224, the page numbers 139 and 174, probably also 176, are recognizable. This indicates that they belonged to a rather large codex. There is, therefore, a fairly large gap between fragments 1 and 2. The name "Jesus" is written twice as a *nomen sacrum* on Fragment 2.

Only remains of letters are preserved on Fragment 1, which do not permit a meaningful reconstruction. Fragment 2 is 6.3 × 13.1 cm in size. From this fragment four small pieces are recognizable, which were originally divided into two columns. Here too, the text is poorly preserved, so that quite a lot must be supplemented. The original sequence of the fragments is uncertain; however, the following sequence is reasonable: recto, column 2—verso, column 1—verso, column 2—recto, column 1. The content of the fragments is as follows. In an appearance, Jesus asks "Why are you disheartened? . . . For not . . .you, but the . . ." Neither the context of this dialogue nor the conversation partner is recognizable. In the next episode, someone apparently asks Jesus what he has rejected and what new teaching and new baptism he proclaims. Here, we appear to be dealing with a controversy between Jesus and a critic of his activity.

In column 2, verso (this would be page 175) scribes, Pharisees (?), and priests get angry about the fact that Jesus (presumably) is reclining at table in the midst of sinners. Jesus reacts to this with the (largely reconstructed) saying, "Those who are healthy have no need of a physician..." Finally (column 1, recto, page 176), we find a few sayings of Jesus in combination: "pray for your enemies," "whoever is not against you is for you," and "They are far away; tomorrow their hour will come." The last saying can no longer be identified.

The fragments exhibit a clear affinity to the Synoptic material and their milieu. The saying about the healthy who do not need a physician has a parallel in Mark 2:17 (and par.); praying for the enemies is related to Jesus' demand to pray for the enemies in the Sermon on the Mount/Plain in Matthew 5:44/Luke 6:27–28 (see also *Didache* 1:3). The saying about being against or for Jesus has a parallel in Mark 9:40 and Luke 9:50. However, a direct literary dependence need not be assumed. The fragments may have belonged to a narrative about Jesus in analogy to the Gospels of the New Testament or P.Egerton 2, dated to the second century. If this were the case, the papyrus would be another piece of evidence for the view that presentations of Jesus' activity arose in the second century alongside the Gospels that were later accepted into the New Testament. However, a more exact reconstruction of the content of the episodes and of the character of the whole text are possible only within limits due to the poor state of preservation. The "appearance of Jesus" is not necessarily to be related to a post-resurrection situation but could also be placed in his earthly activity. The polemical situations as well as the compilation of the different Jewish groups could point to a context in which the profile of the activity of Jesus was given shape in controversies with Judaism. This could point to an origin in the second century CE, but the third century is likewise possible.

Finally, reference may be made to Papyrus Oxyrhynchus 210 from the third century CE. This text contains a few echoes of Jesus traditions, but can be reconstructed only within narrow limits. On the recto the word "angel" can be reconstructed twice (l. 5 and 6), followed by the term "commanded" (l. 4 and 5, partly reconstructed). In l. 7 the word "signs" is perhaps recognizable. It may be that the papyrus contained a story similar to Matthew 1:24 (the command of the angel to Joseph to take Mary as his wife), although the fragmentary character allows only for vague assumptions. On the verso more writing is preserved. Apparently, the text contained the parable about the good tree producing good fruit, followed by an "I am" saying of Jesus. (l. 17–18). In l. 18 the words "I am the image of ..." and in l. 19 "in the form of God" can be identified. Thus, the papyrus apparently contained a speech of Jesus about himself similar to the discourses in the Gospel of John.

The fragments analyzed so far provide information about Jesus traditions beyond and sometimes in relationship to the Gospels that later became part of the New Testament. The literary character of the writings to which these texts belonged is difficult to determine, due to the fragmentary state of the preserved texts. However, it can be inferred that these Jesus traditions were incorporated in writings with biographical character or dialogue form. These fragments, therefore, provide insights in the wide spectrum of interpretations of the person of Jesus and his teaching in early Christianity.

Additions to New Testament Gospels

Stories that were added to the New Testament Gospels in the course of their transmission—i.e., before the textual form stabilized in the fourth century (though it did not become fully uniform even then)—also belong to the texts discussed in this section. Here, we are not dealing with "apocryphal" texts in the literal sense, for the stories were taken up into biblical manuscripts. However, as continuations of the original versions, they belong in the context of the texts that are considered here. Moreover, they indicate that the boundaries between biblical and non-biblical texts are often fluid.

Two prominent examples will be mentioned here (two others will be discussed in Part 5). Codex Cantabrigiensis, a biblical codex from the fifth century, contains the following episode after the narrative of the plucking of grain by the disciples on the Sabbath in the Gospel of Luke (6:1–4): "On the same day, when he saw a certain man working on the Sabbath, he said to him, 'O man, if you know what you are doing, you are blessed; but if you do not know, you are cursed and a transgressor of the Law'" (trans. in "Agrapha," Ehrman and Pleše). In this way, the preceding (and following) episode(s) about the observance of the Sabbath commandment in Luke's Gospel are placed in an altered context. The importance of knowledge of the Sabbath commandment is stressed. Only if one knows what the Sabbath is about is working on the Sabbath— i.e., the non-observance of the strict prohibition of every form of work on the Sabbath—a work that leads to blessedness. In addition, the saying "The Son of Man is Lord over the Sabbath," which concludes the episode about the plucking of grain in the other manuscripts, is placed at the end of both Sabbath episodes (i.e., after v. 10) in Codex Cantabrigiensis.

The Gospel of John contains an episode (7:53–11) about a woman who is caught in the act of adultery and brought to him by scribes and Pharisees. They refer to the law of Moses, according to which the woman is to be stoned. Jesus, however, says in response: "Let anyone among you who is without sin be the first to throw a stone at her." Since no one does this, Jesus also does not condemn the woman, but exhorts her to sin no more. This episode is lacking in the important old manuscripts of John. Thus, it was added only later to the Gospel of John. It is, however, also mentioned in Didymus the Blind. He writes:

> We find, therefore, in certain gospels: A woman, it says, was condemned by the Jews for a sin and was being sent to be stoned in the place where that was customary to happen. The saviour, it says, when he saw her and observed that they were ready to stone her, said to those who were about to cast stones, 'He who has not sinned, let him take a stone and cast it. If anyone is conscious in himself not to have sinned, let him take up a stone and smite her.' And no one dared. Since they knew in themselves and perceived that they themselves were guilty in some things, they did not dare to strike her." (*Comm. Eccl.* 223.6b–13a; trans. Ehrman)

Eusebius, in turn, reports that Papias mentions a story about a woman who is accused before the Lord because of her many sins, though Papias attributes it to the *Gospel according to the Hebrews*:

> And he [Papias] also sets forth another story concerning a woman who was accused of many sins before the Lord, which the Gospel according to the Hebrews contains. (*Hist. eccl.* 3.39.17)

It cannot be clearly determined whether this information is accurate, such that the episode actually occurred in the *Gospel according to the Hebrews*. In any case, it is clear that the story was known in early Christianity and that it was also taken up in the Gospel of John.

Sources and Studies

Bell, H. Idris, and Theodore C. Skeat, eds. *Fragments of an Unknown Gospel and Other Early Christian Papyri*. London: Trustees of the British Museum, 1935.

Ehrman, Bart. "Jesus and the Adulteress." *NTS* 34 (1988) 24–44.

Elliott, J. K., trans. *The Apocryphal New Testament: A Collection of Apocryphal Christian Literature in an English Translation*. Oxford: Oxford University Press, 1993. Rev. repr. 1999 ("Jewish-Christian Gospels," 3–16).

Grenfell, Bernard P., and Arthur S. Hunt, eds. *The Oxyrhynchus Papyri*. London: Egypt Exploration Fund, 1898–1914 (vol. 1 for P.Oxy. 1; vol. 2 for P.Oxy. 210; vol. 4 for P. Oxy. 654 and 655; vol. 5 for P. Oxy. 840; vol. 10 for P.Oxy. 1224).

Izydorczyk, Zbigniew, ed. *Manuscripts of the Evangelium Nicodemi: A Census*. Subsidia Mediaevalia 21. Toronto: Pontifical Institute of Mediaeval Studies, 1993.

———. *The Medieval Gospel of Nicodemus: Texts, Intertexts, and Contexts in Western Europe*. Tempe, AZ: Medieval and Renaissance Texts & Studies, 1997.

Kraus, Thomas J., Michael J. Kruger, and Tobias Nicklas, eds. and trans. *Gospel Fragments*. Oxford Early Christian Gospel Texts. Oxford: Oxford University Press, 2009.

Kruger, Michael J. *The Gospel of the Savior: An Analysis of P.Oxy. 840 and Its Place in the Gospel Traditions of Early Christianity*. TENTS 1. Leiden: Brill, 2005.

Landau, Brent C., and Stanley E. Porter. "Papyrus Oxyrhynchus 210: A New Translation and Introduction." In *New Testament Apocrypha: More Noncanonical Scriptures*, vol. 1, edited by Tony Burke and Brent Landau, 107–22. Grand Rapids, MI: Eerdmans, 2016.

Lührmann, Dieter. *Fragmente apokryph gewordener Evangelien: In griechischer und lateinischer Sprache*. Marburg: Elwert, 2000.

Rees, Brinley R.. "51. Christian Fragment." In *A Descriptive Catalogue of the Greek Papyri in the Collection of Wilfred Merton, F.S.A.*, vol. 2, edited by Brinley R. Rees, H. Idris Bell, and John W. B. Barns, 1–4. 3 vols. Dublin: Hodges Figgis, 1948–1967.

Zelyck, Lorne R. *The Egerton Gospel (Egerton Papyrus 2 + P. Köln VI 255): Introduction, Critical Edition, and Commentary*. TENTS 13. Leiden: Brill, 2019.

4

Traditions about the Suffering and Death of Jesus

Introduction

A GROUP OF APOCRYPHAL writings take the passion narratives of the New Testament Gospels as their starting point and then present the suffering and death of Jesus in their own way. Some of these texts are only fragmentarily extant, so that one can no longer say what scope and literary character the complete texts had. Nevertheless, it is possible to recognize tendencies within the interpretation of the passion of Jesus. The situation is different in the case of the *Gospel of Judas* and the *Gospel of Nicodemus*. From the outset, these two writings were oriented—in rather different ways—to the interpretation of the passion of Jesus. The following section will treat both fragmentary texts as well as those for which the literary and content-related profile is recognizable. It will become clear that, from the earliest times, Jesus' suffering and death formed an important area for interpreting his work.

The *Gospel of Peter*

A "Gospel of Peter" is mentioned already by ancient Christian theologians. Here, the letter of bishop Serapion is of special interest. In this letter, which was originally composed around 180 CE and subsequently handed down by Eusebius (*Eccl. hist.* 6.12.3–6, see the quotation above in the Introduction), Serapion writes to the community at Rhossos, whom he had visited shortly before. During this visit, some of the members of the community presented him with a gospel issued under the name of Peter. At first, Serapion, not having much knowledge of the text, declared that it may be read. Subsequently, however, he learned that the community members in question were inclined to a heresy. Therefore, he says he will visit the community again soon. In addition, through others who used this gospel, he has become more familiar with it. He has determined that most of what is in it corresponds to the true teaching of the Savior but that some things deviate from it. The quotation of the letter breaks off at this point. Thus, Eusebius does not hand down what Serapion thought these deviant teachings were. At best, the statement that some of those who used this gospel "are called by us docetists" could provide a clue. However, this only informs us about how the group that used this gospel is designated by Serapion and others, it does not give us information about their self-understanding, let alone about the *Gospel of Peter*.

The correspondence shows that at the time of Serapion it was apparently not uncommon for other gospels than the four already recognized Gospels to be read in a Christian community. Thus, the emergence of the four-Gospel collection did not mean that other gospels would have been unknown. Rather, precisely in light of the multiplicity of gospels and other writings, early Christian theologians attempted to develop criteria for distinguishing between recognized and rejected writings. In the process, the apocryphal writings did not automatically disappear from the stock of writings used for reading in the community and in private. Moreover, the boundaries between biblical and non-biblical writings were fluid for quite some time, being drawn more clearly only in the fourth century CE. It is not surprising, therefore, that Serapion, at his first visit, saw no reason to prohibit the reading of *Peter* in the community. Only its use by a group that was classified as "heretical"—i.e., that, in his view, advocated teachings that endangered the unity of the community—caused him to prohibit the reading of the work. What Serapion read in *Peter* and, in particular, what moved him to revise his initial judgment, can no longer be determined.

A text that has been identified by scholars as the "Gospel according to Peter" has been known since the end of the nineteenth century. In winter 1886/1887 a parchment codex was discovered in a cemetery near Akhmîm in Upper Egypt; it was published in 1892 by Urbain Bouriant. The first five sheets of the codex contain the work that is called the *Gospel of Peter* today. It is a fragment of a more extensive narrative. This is already recognizable from the fact that the text begins in the middle of a sentence and also ends with an incomplete sentence. It is evident that the scribe only knew this section of the text, as shown by ornaments and decorations at the beginning and end of the manuscript.

The codex, which also contains two additional writings—the Greek *Apocalypse of Peter* (on this text, see the section below) and part of Greek *Enoch*—dates from the sixth or seventh century. The writings themselves, however, are older. We cannot say with certainty whether the first writing is to be identified with the text referred to in the aforementioned letter of Serapion. In light of the temporal distance of several centuries, it would be somewhat reckless to assume an identical text. This applies, first, insofar as we must reckon with revisions and modifications, which were probably more extensive for non-biblicals text than with biblical texts, since the latter were already subject to a stronger standardization due to their use in liturgical and other ecclesial contexts. Second, the Akhmîm fragment has no title, so that the assignment to the *Gospel of Peter* can be deduced only from internal indications. Here, the starting point is the fact that a first-person narrator appears twice in the text. In the first place, it says, "But I and my companions were grieving ..." (26). This is a statement of one of the disciples of Jesus after the death and burial of Jesus. At the end of the fragment it then says: "But I, Simon Peter, and my brother Andrew ..." (60). The narrator is thus identified by name here. On the basis of these two texts, the work can be assigned to (pseudonymous) "Peter." Since it is a (fragmentary) story of Jesus, it is probable that we are dealing with the same writing that Serapion mentions, even though we must assume that there have been developments in the textual form between the second and sixth/seventh centuries CE.

In addition to the Akhmîm fragment, several other manuscripts have been assigned to the *Gospel of Peter*. P.Oxy. 2949, which was edited by R. A. Coles in 1972, consists of two fragments written on one side only, with thirteen and five lines of text respectively. The papyrus is dated to the late second or early third century, so that it would be an early witness for the existence of *Peter*. While only a few words or letters are preserved, they nevertheless allow a connection to the Akhmîm fragment to be established. The reconstruction shows, however, that they are not simply identical texts; rather, the papyrus attests its own version of the text. P.Oxy. 2949 does not expand our knowledge of the content of *Peter* beyond what is known from the Akhmîm text. Another papyrus that has been brought into connection with *Peter* is P.Oxy. 4009. It is a papyrus page written on both sides with 21 or 20 lines of text, though only a few letters or words are preserved from each line. This could allow a reconstruction of a dialogue between Jesus and a first-person narrator in which Jesus gives an exhortation to fearless confession. In 2 *Clement*, which probably arose in the middle of the second century CE, we find a similar dialogue between Jesus and Peter, who is mentioned by name in the third person:

> For the Lord says, "You will be like lambs among wolves." But Peter answered and said to him, "What if the wolves tear the lambs to pieces?" Jesus said to Peter, "After the lambs are dead, let them fear the wolves no longer, and as for you, do not fear those who, though they kill you, are not able to do anything else to you, but fear the one who, after you are dead, has the power to cast soul and body into the flames of hell." (5.2–4; trans. Holmes)

Dieter Lührmann has concluded from this that the dialogue from P.Oxy. 4009 could be assigned to *Peter*, since it is configured as a first-person narration of Peter. In that case, the scene could either be placed right before the passion events or, alternatively, configured as a dialogue of the Risen One with Peter. To be sure, it remains controversial whether the appearance of the first-person narrator is sufficient to assign the Akhmîm text and P.Oxy. 4009 to the same writing. If this is assumed, the textual content of *Peter* would be expanded by a dialogue of Jesus with Peter. Finally, P.Vindob. G 2325 (the so-called Fayûm Fragment) has been brought into connection with *Peter*. Since, however, the indicators for an assignment to *Peter* are even weaker and are indeed doubtful (the identity of the first-person narrator is not preserved on the fragment and must be inferred as Peter through a reconstruction that is by no means certain), this fragment will be discussed in its own section.

The Akhmîm text contains a distinct version of the passion narrative. It is no longer possible to determine how extensive the writing was originally—i.e., whether it was a gospel that also contained traditions about the activity of Jesus prior to his passion. The New Testament Gospels are apparently presupposed in *Peter*, with particularly clear echoes of Matthew and Luke; however, it offers a distinct interpretation of the condemnation, crucifixion, and resurrection of Jesus. The text's main characteristics are its negative presentation of the role of the Jews and its graphic portrayal of the resurrection of Jesus. The text could belong, therefore, in a context in which the resurrection of Jesus was defended through a graphic narrative in the face of its contestation by Jews and gentiles. At the same time, the presentation of the Jews could point to a situation of estrangement and hostility between Jews and Christians. Since *Peter* probably arose in the second century, such a situation would need to be sought within this time period, without it being possible to specify this more exactly in time or location.

The Akhmîm text begins in the middle of a sentence that had apparently begun with Pilate washing his hands in a display of innocence during the trial (cf. Matthew 27:24). The following continuation is then preserved: "... But none of the Jews washed his hands, nor did Herod or any of his judges" (1). The "Herod" in view is Herod Antipas, who also appears in the passion narrative of the Gospel of Luke (23:6–12). The author of *Peter*, however, does not possess more exact knowledge of the historical circumstances, for shortly thereafter he calls Herod "king" and notes that he had given the order to lead away the Lord. Moreover, the request of Joseph (of Arimathea) to be permitted to bury the body of the Lord after the crucifixion is transferred from Pilate to Herod, who answers that "we" would bury him anyway due to the beginning of the Sabbath. These details clearly contradict the political realities, for Antipas neither bore the title of "king" (in contrast to Herod the Great, during whose reign Jesus was born) nor did he have authority to give orders in Jerusalem. The characterization of "Herod" as a Jew may have been inferred from the New Testament Gospels, which depict Herod the Great and Herod Antipas as Jews as well.

The subsequent course of the narrative portrays how Jesus is mocked and crucified between two criminals. The leaders of the Jews—called scribes, Pharisees, and elders—recognize that they have incurred guilt and become afraid because the people regard Jesus as a righteous man. Therefore, they ask Pilate to have guards watch the tomb of Joseph (of Arimathea), where Jesus was buried, for three days, so that his disciples do not steal the corpse, leading people to believe that he is risen from the dead (cf. Matthew 28:11–15). This is followed by a very detailed portrayal of the resurrection of Jesus:

> But during the night on which the Lord's day dawned, while the soldiers stood guard two by two on their watch, a great voice came from the sky. They saw the skies open and two men descend from there; they were very bright and drew near to the tomb. That stone which had been cast before the entrance rolled away by itself and moved to one side; the tomb was open and

TRADITIONS ABOUT THE SUFFERING AND DEATH OF JESUS

> both young men entered. When the soldiers saw these things, they woke up the centurion and the elders—for they were also there on guard. As they were explaining what they had seen, they saw three men emerge from the tomb, two of them supporting the other, with a cross following behind them. The heads of the two reached up to the sky, but the head of the one they were leading went up above the skies. And they heard a voice from the skies, "Have you preached to those who are asleep?" And a reply came from the cross, "Yes." (35–42)

The scene portrays the resurrection of Jesus in a way that clearly goes beyond the New Testament Gospels. They report only the discovery of the empty tomb and the appearances of the Risen One, but not the resurrection itself.

The resurrection scene is followed by the account of Mary Magdalene's visit to the tomb, together with her friends. *Peter* explicitly mentions that due to fear of the Jews, Mary had not done for the corpse of the Lord what women customarily do for the dead—namely, anoint it for burial. The last scene presents the resurrection message that a young man directs to the women. The women then become afraid and flee, while "we, the twelve disciples of the Lord," went home in grief (58–59). This is followed by the sentence "But I, Simon Peter, and my brother Andrew, took our nets and went to the sea. And with us was Levi, the son of Alphaeus, whom the Lord . . ." (60). At this point the fragment breaks off.

Thus, what is characteristic for *Peter* is, first, the further development of features of the passion story through a vivid portrayal of the resurrection—in a sense as a counterpart to the drastic portrayal of the virgin birth in the *Protevangelium* and its later adaptions—and through the emphasis upon the guilt of the Jewish people for the death of Jesus. The Jewish people appear as the main actors of the mocking and crucifixion of Jesus, though they are not aware of what they do and downright symbolically stumble about in the dark in the middle of the day (18). Thus, *Peter* can be understood as a creative reinterpretation of the passion story during a time when the tensions between Christian and Jews had begun to intensify.

The *Gospel of Judas*

The *Gospel of* (not: according to) *Judas* is the apocryphal gospel that has most recently become known. It was published in 2007 by Rudolphe

Kasser and Gregor Wurst as the third work in a codex with a total of five works in the Coptic language. The codex circulated for about two years on the antiquities market in different countries before it was finally purchased in 2000 by the Swiss collector Frieda Nussberger-Tchacos, for which reason it is called "Codex Tchacos." During this time, it was severely damaged, which made an extensive reconstruction necessary. This began in 2001 and continued even after the original publication in 2007.

The two works that precede *Judas* also appear in the codices from Nag Hammadi—i.e., they were already known prior to the publication of Codex Tchacos. The works in question are the *Letter of Peter to Philip* (also in NHC VII,2) and the *First Apocalypse of James* (also in NHC V,3). The two writings that follow *Judas* are only preserved in fragments. One is a previously unknown writing, in which a figure called Allogenes plays a central role. The other is another writing that belongs to the gnostic stream of the Hermetics. All the writings are Coptic translations of texts originally written in Greek.

A "Gospel of Judas" is already mentioned by Irenaeus. In his work *Against Heresies*, he writes:

> And others say that Cain was from the superior realm of absolute power, and confess that Esau, Korah, the Sodomites, and all such persons are of the same people (or nation) as themselves; for this reason they have been hated by their maker, although none of them has suffered harm. For wisdom (Sophia) snatched up out of them whatever of them belonged to her. And furthermore—they say—Judas the betrayer was thoroughly acquainted with these things; and he alone was acquainted with the truth as no others were, and (so) accomplished the mystery of the betrayal. By him all things, both earthly and heavenly, were thrown into dissolution. And they bring forth a fabricated work to this effect, which they entitle *The Gospel of Judas*. (Haer. 1.31.1; trans. Pearson)

Thus, Irenaeus knows that *Judas* is used by groups who advocate a distinctive myth about God, the world, and salvation. This myth is only hinted at here, whereas it is developed in greater detail in other gnostic writings. According to the note in Irenaeus, the aforementioned groups appeal to figures that play a negative role in Genesis—Cain, for the murder of his brother, Esau, as the deceiver, etc. Judas, who handed over Jesus, also belongs in this series. The provocation of *Judas* consists in the fact that it makes Judas, of all people, the protagonist and eponym of a gospel.

Furthermore, an opposition between the Creator and Sophia is recognizable. The Creator—a negative figure—treats the aforementioned persons with hostility, whereas Sophia takes to herself what belongs to her from them—i.e., presumably their souls.

In his large work, Irenaeus engages critically with such doctrinal systems, which he apparently knows well. Before the discovery of the Nag Hammadi writings, Irenaeus was, therefore, a main source for our knowledge of ancient "gnosis"—an umbrella term for different systems that share a number of characteristics, such as the radical opposition between the highest, good God and the material world; the existence of diverse mediating figures or entities between God and world and especially of a jealous creator god, who can also be called "demiurge"; and the salvation from this prison through knowledge ("gnosis"), which teaches humans about their kinship with the upper sphere and is mediated by a figure from the upper sphere. Salvation consists in the liberation of the soul from the prison of the material body and its ascent through different spheres extending to the highest God. The gnostic systems existed in different forms. Sometimes only individual features are mentioned, behind which a more comprehensive myth stands. Sometimes only individual aspects play a role, without it being possible to characterize the writing in question as "gnostic." Moreover, there are various connections between "gnostic" and "Christian" writings (though sometimes also clear contradictions), so that it is not always possible to draw clear boundaries.

Only a few of the elements mentioned in the passage quoted from Irenaeus appear in *Judas*. The names Cain, Esau, etc., which he quotes, play no role in the writing, and Sophia is mentioned only in passing. Irenaeus apparently does not have exact knowledge of the writing but knows only that certain groups appeal to it. However, the statement that Judas "performed the mystery of the handing over" and the statement about the "dissolution of the earthly and heavenly things" are quite compatible with *Judas*.

At the beginning, the writing is characterized as "the hidden word of revelation that Jesus spoke with Judas Iscariot in the course of eight days, three days before he celebrated Passover." The content of Jesus' speech to Judas is thus characterized as "hidden" ("apocryphal"). This also appears in other writings. The specification of time refers to the weeks before the Passover on which Jesus was crucified (thus according to the Synoptic Gospels; according to the Gospel of John, the crucifixion took place on the day before Passover). The following encounters thus occur prior to the crucifixion and take place on multiple successive days.

At the outset, there is a report of a meeting of Jesus with his disciples. The disciples are presented here as uncomprehending and giving thanks to another god, about which Jesus laughs. A special role is assigned to Judas. He is the only one who recognizes where Jesus has come from—namely, "from the immortal aeon of Barbelo" (35,17–18). The name Barbelo occurs in multiple gnostic writings as a designation for the (often feminine) divine principle, which belongs to the upper sphere and is assigned to the highest, invisible spirit (see the discussion of the *Apocryphon of John* below). Both Irenaeus and Epiphanius report about people who worship Barbelo and are designated, therefore, as "Barbeliotes." It is uncertain where the name comes from and what it means. It often plays a role in gnostic writings.

In *Judas*, Jesus announces that he is going to communicate "the mysteries of the kingdom" to Judas, due to his ability to recognize Jesus' origins. Moreover, Jesus tells Judas that someone else will take his place in order that the number of the twelve disciples can be complete again. Thus, *Judas* presupposes the tradition of the circle of twelve disciples and the tradition of the replacement of Judas through another disciple (cf. Acts 1:15–26).

In another dialogue, Jesus speaks to his disciples about the "great (or, alternatively, strong) holy generation," which does not originate from those who are mortal (35,23–34) . This allusion to a gnostic myth is developed further at a later point in the work. Jesus teaches Judas about "the generation that will endure" and whose souls remain alive. Before Judas is initiated further into this myth, sacrificial rituals and the temple cult are criticized. The disciples tell Jesus about a vision in which they saw priests present offerings; others even offered their own children or made themselves guilty of other shameful acts, such as sexual aberrations or murder. Here, a Christian practice oriented to rituals is apparently distorted (38,1–39,3).

Judas is then initiated into the character of the upper world (47,2–53,7). Here, it is possible to recognize elements of the myth that is presented in greater detail in the *Apocryphon of John* (see below). *Judas* mentions the "Great Invisible Spirit," which exists in the "eternal age" and produces from itself other emanations ("things brought forth," "outflows"). Autogenes and Adamas, from whom the "incorruptible generation of Seth" comes forth, belong to the upper world. Because the figure of Seth, the third son of Adam and Eve (after Cain and Abel), plays a central role in some writings, this form of the gnostic myth is sometimes designated as "Sethian Gnosticism." Seth, however, is not a constitutive figure of the myth and can also take up different roles in other writings. Accordingly, it is more appropriate to speak of a "basic form" of the gnostic myth. In this, "the generation that does not waver," which is also called the "generation of perfect human beings," plays an important role. It consists of those who belong to the upper sphere and to whom the teaching about the upper world is imparted. Only the one who belongs to the "unshakeable generation" of Seth will be saved.

In *Judas*, Seth is identified with Jesus Christ—as in the "Egyptian Gospel" from Nag Hammadi (NHC III,2), with which the myth recounted in *Judas* displays quite a few commonalities. The myth also includes a multiplicity of "luminaries," who constitute the world of the upper aeons. The lower world, by contrast, emerges through the fallen angel Nebro, who is called "Yaldabaoth," and through Saklas and the twelve archons. They create Adam and Eve from whom the mortal generation of human beings comes forth, who will serve Saklas. God, however, has caused knowledge to be given to Adam and his people so that the rulers of the underworld have no power over them.

At the end Jesus speaks about himself to Judas (56,11–20). The earthly human being who carries him (Jesus) will be tortured. Judas will sacrifice this human being—i.e., he will hand over the mortal human being Jesus, who is different from his heavenly mode of existence. After this, Judas sees a luminous cloud into which Jesus enters. Then follows a short conclusion that recounts the handing over of Jesus by Judas, for which he receives money (58,19–26).

Judas thus interprets the story of Judas's betrayal in a quite distinct way. The main content of the writing is the myth of the emergence of the upper and the lower worlds, which has close points of contact with the form that also appears in other writings, including the *Apocryphon of John*. Here, this myth is revealed to Judas, though this does not prevent him from sacrificing the earthly human being Jesus. In this respect he behaves in the same way as the disciples criticized at the outset and as the sacrificing priests who are presented as shameful. Indeed, he is presented as even worse, for he sacrifices Christ as an incarnation of Seth. By contrast, the incorruptible nature of Jesus, which belongs to the upper sphere, goes into the heavenly world.

The "Unknown Berlin Gospel"

This writing is attested by a poorly preserved parchment codex from the sixth century, which was purchased in 1967 by the Berlin Egyptian Museum. What remains of the codex is two double pages, two single pages, and twenty-eight small fragments. The page numbers 99/100 and 107/108 are preserved, which points to a large codex. We can no longer determine which writings appeared in this codex and how long the work was that is now called the *Unknown Berlin Gospel* (whether this title is appropriate, however, may be disputed since the writing may belong to another kind of literature). The codex was discovered in 1991 by Paul Mirecki in the Berlin Museum and first made accessible in 1998 through the German translation of Hans-Martin Schenke. The year after, Mirecki, together with Charles W. Hedrick, presented an initial (though flawed) edition under the title *Gospel of the Savior*. Another German translation by Uwe-Karsten Plisch followed in 2000. Most recently, Alin Suciu has published a new edition and translation of the text. He argues that the text is an original Coptic composition that shares literary features with a range of other Coptic texts, all created, it seems, in the fifth century or later.

Soon after the text's publication in 1998, connections between the *Unknown Berlin Gospel* and the Strasbourg Coptic Papyrus (see below) were recognized. Moreover, connections to the *Gospel of Peter* were postulated, though these remain uncertain. It is possible, however, to establish a proximity to the Gospel of John, with which it has points of contact in a number of features.

The text consists of dialogues of Jesus—who is usually called "the Savior"—with his disciples, though only Andrew and John are mentioned by name. It begins in the middle of a saying of Jesus about the "kingdom of heaven." In the further course of the work, Jesus exhorts them to leave "this place," because the person who will hand him over is drawing near (cf. Mark 14:42).

The dialogues that follow present an analogy to the farewell discourses of the Gospel of John, as Jesus prepares the disciples for the fact that he will be with them only for a short time yet. Here, we find close connections to the Gospel of John, such as in the statement "I and my Father, we are a single one" (cf. John 10:30) or in the interpretation of the death of Jesus: He will, as the good shepherd, give his life for the disciples (cf. John 10:11). This is connected with the exhortation that the disciples should also give their lives for their friends (cf. 1 John 3:16) and developed further through the fact that Jesus gives his life for human beings (cf. John 10:11; 15:13). There are, however, also connections to extra-canonical sayings of Jesus, such as:

> "If someone approaches me, he will [burn]. I am the [fire that] blazes. The [one who draws] close to me, draws close to [the] fire, the one who is far from me is far from life." (107,43–48; trans. Suciu)

This saying appears in a similar form in the *Gospel of Thomas* (82) as well as in Origen and Didymus the Blind. In the *Unknown Berlin Gospel*, these traditions are joined in a distinct way into a presentation of Jesus as incarnate God, who clarifies the meaning of his death for his disciples.

In addition, a version of the transfiguration story is presented (100–103). The disciples are transfigured together with Jesus and experience a heavenly journey in which they encounter doorkeepers, angels, archangels, and cherubim who lead them before the throne of the Father. This is followed by an interesting version of the Gethsemane scene from the Synoptic Gospels, though here Jesus is not tormented by fear, rather his sorrow has a different reason—namely, the fate of Israel. Jesus petitions the Father multiple times that the cup may pass him by. The reason for this is that Jesus wishes to be killed by a different sinful people and not by Israel. This presupposes the view that Jesus was killed by the Jews, which is also represented by other writings, such as the *Gospel of Peter*. At the same time, the solidarity of Jesus with Israel is expressed, especially when he contrasts the people of Israel with the sinful nations and calls Abraham, Isaac, and Jacob "his beloved."

Finally, Jesus makes an address to the cross (106–12). Here, a distinction is made between one Jesus, who laughs and rejoices, and another, who weeps and laments—presumably a division between the earthly Jesus and the heavenly, as also found in the *Gospel of Judas* and in other early Christian writings. The independent significance that the cross receives through the address of Jesus is also notable. Here again there is an analogy with the *Gospel of Peter*, where the cross follows Jesus out of the grave, and is thus similarly nearly personified.

Despite its fragmentary state of preservation, the *Unknown Berlin Gospel* displays a distinct presentation of the passion events. Through the dialogue with the disciples right before the crucifixion, Jesus' suffering and death receive a deeper interpretation. In addition to the connections to the Synoptic Gospels, the intensive use of the Gospel of John, to which it is also close in content, is conspicuous. The text may be regarded as an example of "Apostolic Memoirs," a genre proposed by Alin Suciu for texts which were composed in Coptic and reflect the alienation of the church of Egypt from the Byzantine church. The "Apostolic Memoirs" are pseudonymous writings of the apostles which were often framed by sermons of the church fathers. Another example of this genre would be the *History of Joseph the Carpenter* discussed above.

The Strasbourg Coptic Papyrus

The papyrus consists of two pages, written on both sides, of a very fragmentarily preserved codex, which dates from the fifth or sixth century. Since 1899 they have been owned by the Strasbourg National and University Library (designated as Kopt. 5 and Kopt. 6) and were published in a definitive edition by Carl Schmidt in 1900. The page numbers 157 and 158 can be recognized on the second page. As especially Stephen Emmel has pointed out, the fragments display a clear affinity to the *Unknown Berlin Gospel*. Emmel's observations are supported by Alin Suciu who provided more arguments that the two texts belonged to the same writing, which he dubs "The Berlin-Strasbourg Apocryphon."

On the front side, the first page contains a prayer of Jesus to the Father, in which Jesus, among other things, says that God will subject all things to him, and that the adversary and the sting of death will be destroyed. These are clear echoes of 1 Corinthians 15. On the back, there is a variant of the Gethsemane episode. Jesus turns to his disciples and speaks of the approaching hour of his being taken away (cf. Mark 14:41//Matthew 26:45). Moreover, we find the saying "the spirit is willing, but the flesh is weak" (cf. Mark 14:38//Matthew 26:41). Jesus strengthens the apostles with the pronouncement that earthly enemies have power only over their body. On Kopt. 6, recto, it is perhaps possible to reconstruct the statement that Jesus will reveal his glory to the disciples. On the back, the apostles confess that they saw "the glory of his deity" and were entrusted with the power of the office of apostle. Thus, the papyrus was apparently part of a farewell scene of Jesus, as it also appears in the *Unknown Berlin Gospel*. It may be concluded, therefore, that we are dealing with two manuscripts of the same writing.

Papryrus Vindobonensis G 2325 (Fayûm Fragment)

The small fragment (3.5 × 4.3 cm), written on one side, belongs to the collection of the Austrian National Library and presumably comes from the Fayûm (Heracleopolis) in Upper Egypt. It was first published by G. Bickell in 1885 and dates from the third century CE. The text contains a speech of Jesus to his disciples in which he announces to them that they will take offence "in this (?) night"; what is meant is apparently the night of the arrest and trial of Jesus. This is grounded with a scriptural quotation that is also found in Mark 14:27 and Matthew 26:31: "I will strike the shepherd and the sheep will be scattered" (cf. Zechariah 13:7). Peter (the name is written as a *nomen sacrum* "PET") answers: "Even if all do so, I will not." This is followed by Jesus' prophecy of Peter's denial. We are thus dealing with a fragment that contains an episode from the passion narratives of the Synoptic Gospels (Mark 14:26–31//Matthew 26:30–35, somewhat differently Luke 22:31–34). The relationship to these can scarcely be determined clearly.

As mentioned above, Dieter Lührman brought the fragment into connection with the *Gospel of Peter*. To do so, Lührmann fills in a gap in line 5 in such a way that Peter appears as a first-person narrator: "As I, Peter, said . . .". This addition, however, is very improbable. It should read: "Peter said . . .". But with this the decisive argument for assigning it to the *Gospel of Peter* falls away. The writing to which the fragment belonged can no longer be determined.

The *Gospel of Nicodemus* / The *Acts of Pilate*

The *Gospel of Nicodemus* focuses exclusively on the events of the passion and resurrection. The writing was composed in Greek, where it goes by the title *Acts of Pilate*, and then translated into Latin, as the *Gospel of Nicodemus*, and numerous other languages. It has developed an extremely rich influence that extends into the present, for example, in the shaping of passion plays and in literary presentations of the passion of Jesus; its impact is signaled not least by the considerable number of more than 500 manuscripts in which it is extant. A significant reason for this popularity is the colorful elaboration of the passion and resurrection events, including Christ's descent into hell. *Nicodemus* can be viewed, therefore, as a counterpart to the Infancy Gospels. It makes clear that, in a way comparable to his birth and childhood, the suffering and death of Jesus had great significance for Christian piety from the beginning and were correspondingly embellished.

It is not by chance that, like the Infancy Gospels, *Nicodemus* has an extremely complex tradition history. The earliest part (chaps. 1 to 16) probably goes back to the second century, as is suggested by the testimonies discussed below. This part is usually called today "Acts of Pilate A" (distinct from the "Acts of Pilate B," on which see below). The A-text is preserved in a Greek and a Latin version with different designations of the writing. The prologue of the Greek version speaks of the "records ... of our Lord Jesus Christ, which the Jews have composed under Pontius Pilate" in Hebrew and which were allegedly translated into Greek by Ananias, a Roman bodyguard with the rank of officer who became a Christian and presents himself as the pseudonymous author of the text. In the Latin version, by contrast, the writing is designated as "deeds and actions of our Lord and Savior Jesus Christ," which were allegedly found "in the praetorium of Pontius Pilate, in the public archives." Moreover, both prologues refer to written records of Nicodemus in Hebrew, which are said to contain the passion events. This at least stands in tension with the "records" composed by the Jews of the Greek prologue. According to the Gospel of John (19:38–42), Nicodemus was present at the entombment of Jesus and can, therefore, be regarded as a witness of the trial against Jesus and the events that follow, which explains the attribution of the writing to him.

For the first part (chapters 1–16) the title "Gesta Pilati" ("Acts/Deeds of Pilate") is also attested, which is reflected in the aforementioned specifications of the prologue. It recounts the trial against Jesus in which Nicodemus and some other Jews stand up for Jesus, then the crucifixion and burial of Jesus (chaps. 1–11), followed by the imprisonment of Joseph of Arimathea, his liberation through divine intervention, and further events related to Joseph (chaps. 12–16). The latter part may have been added to the actual "Acts of Pilate" at a second stage in the development of the textual tradition. In the B-text (in Tischendorf's edition "Evangelii Nicodemi Pars Altera") the story continues with an account of the descent of Christ into the underworld (17–27). Various manuscripts contain, in addition, diverse continuations. These point toward the extensive Pilate literature, including various fictive letters from Pilate to the emperor Claudius and to the tetrarch Herod, to Pilate from the emperor Tiberius and from Herod, as well as the "Martyrdom of Pilate" and a related text called the "Lament of the Virgin."

TRADITIONS ABOUT THE SUFFERING AND DEATH OF JESUS

The origin of the tradition history of *Nicodemus* lies in speculations about actual acts of the trial against Jesus. Already in the middle of the second century CE, in Justin's *First Apology*—a defense of Christianity addressed to the Roman emperor—we find a note about "acts produced under Pontius Pilate." These are purported to record the process of the crucifixion of Jesus as it is also portrayed in the Gospels (35.9). At a later point, Justin notes that the healings of Jesus are also recorded in these acts (48.3). About fifty years later, Tertullian, in his *Apologeticum*, says that Pilate, who is said to have been "himself a Christian in the innermost being," instructed the Emperor Tiberius about Jesus' activity in Galilee, his crucifixion, resurrection, and ascension to heaven (21.24). However, Tertullian does not mention any official acts of the trial. This tradition is taken up by Eusebius in the fourth century (*Hist. eccl.* 1.9.3–4; 9.5.1; 9.7.1). He also knows of "Acts of Pilate," which are said to have been discovered and circulated by pagans at the time of Emperor Maximinus Daia (died in 311) in order to defame "our Savior." Epiphanius then presupposes the existence of Christian acts of Pilate later in the fourth century (*Pan.* 50.1).

Are the Christian *Acts of Pilate*, therefore, an invention as a reaction to the pagan acts? And are those likewise invented? The situation is probably more complex. More recent scholarship on the *Acts of Pilate* suggests that we are dealing with a work from the second century CE in which Jewish objections against Jesus were formulated. This fits with the aforementioned note in the Greek prologue of *Nicodemus* about the acts composed by the Jews. Later, the work was then reworked further and used against the Christian faith by pagans. On the Christian side, the acts of Pilate—which are in any case a legend and not actual acts of the trial—were then revised and joined with the other parts of *Nicodemus* mentioned above.

Thus, the Christian *Acts of Pilate* probably arose in the fourth century and in the first half of the fifth century were furnished with the prologue (or prologues) and successively placed together with the other parts. This can also be connected with the specifications of time in the prologue; while these differ among one another, an origin account of this sort is nevertheless suggested by them.

Nicodemus begins with accusations that the Jews make against Jesus before Pilate. According to them, he claims to be Son of God and king, profanes the Sabbath, and wants to abolish the Jewish law. Later the accusation is added that he was born from fornication, though this is disputed by other Jews. Pilate doubts these accusations and interrogates

Jesus. Some of the Jews, however, vehemently demand the execution of Jesus, whereas Nicodemus defends Jesus before Pilate by presenting his objections, which he also brought forward before the Jews. Some of the people who were healed by Jesus also support him by recounting that he healed them, including the woman with a blood flow, who bears the name Berenice, which corresponds to the Latin "Veronica" (7). Finally, Pilate can no longer withstand the anger of the Jews and hands Jesus over to be crucified. Joseph of Arimathea asks for the corpse of Jesus and buries him in a rock-hewn tomb.

In the next part (12–15), the Jews have Joseph thrown into prison as revenge for the fact that he buried Jesus and makes accusations against them. When they go to interrogate him, they find the prison empty. The guards of the tomb of Jesus also report experiencing an earthquake and seeing an angel who proclaimed the resurrection of Jesus. After the Sanhedrin's attempt to spread the rumor that the corpse of Jesus was stolen fails, and additional witnesses of the resurrection turn up, Joseph is brought back from Galilee to Jerusalem, where he is received by Nicodemus into his house. He tells the Sanhedrin about his miraculous liberation from prison. The Jews who had previously rejected Jesus and his message are convinced by the unified witness to the resurrection of Jesus and ultimately confess it (16).

Christ's "Descent to Hades" is connected to what precedes it through the fact that it is presented as a report of Joseph. He points to the fact that not only Christ, but also many others, including the two sons of Simeon, who was mentioned earlier and who appears in the birth story of the Gospel of Luke (2:25–35), were raised from the dead. The two sons write down their experiences in the underworld. According to their account, they saw, together with Abraham, a great light, about which Isaiah had already spoken (Isa 9:1–2). John the Baptist is present and even in death, continues to testify for Jesus. Seth, the son of Adam, testifies that at the gates to paradise he received the prophecy that the Son of God would descend to the underworld 5500 years after the creation of the world. There is a conversation between Satan and Hades about the reception of Jesus into the underworld; they are interrupted by a voice that exhorts them to open the doors of the underworld so that the king of glory may enter. Jesus enters, binds Satan, and liberates Adam and the rest of the prisoners. He leads them to paradise where they are received by the archangel Michael. Enoch and Elijah are also there, as is the robber named Dysmas who was crucified with Jesus and to whom Jesus had promised that he would be with him in paradise (Luke 23:43).

Nicodemus is a work as complex as it was influential. It was repeatedly updated and continued to shape the perception of the passion of Jesus into the Middle Ages. An early German prose translation (14th century) can be found in the *Klosterneuburger Evangelienwerk*, a Gospel Harmony which contains several apocryphal episodes about the birth and childhood of Jesus, along with chapters from the medieval compilation *The Golden Legend*, and the *Gospel of Nicodemus*. Another translation was included in the *Augsburger Bibelhandschrift* from 1350 as well as in other Bible translations, sometimes with the remark that it does not belong to the Bible. In the modern period, the influence of *Nicodemus* receded with the rise of historical criticism, which especially rejected the part about Christ in Hades.

Sources and Studies

Bickell, G. "Ein Papyrusfragment eines nichtkanonischen Evangeliums." *ZKT* 9 (1885) 498–504.

Bouriant, Urbain. "Fragments du texte grec du livre d'Énoch et de quelques écrits attribués à saint Pierre." In *Mémoires publiées par les membres de la mission archéologique française au Caire* 9, 93–147. Paris: Leroux, 1892.

Coles, R. Alan, ed. "2949. Fragments of an Apocryphal Gospel (?)." In *The Oxyrhynchus Papyri*, vol. 41, edited by Gerald M. Browne, 15–16. London: Egypt Exploration Society, 1972.

Ehrman, Bart D. *The Lost Gospel of Judas Iscariot: A New Look at Betrayer and Betrayed*. Oxford: Oxford University Press, 2006.

Emmel, Stephen. "The Recently Published *Gospel of the Savior* ('Unbekanntes Berliner Evangelium'): Righting the Order of Pages and Events." *HTR* 95 (2002) 45–72.

———. "Unbekanntes Berliner Evangelium = The Strasbourg Coptic Gospel: Prolegomena to a New Edition of the Strasbourg Fragments." In *For the Children Perfect Instruction: Studies in Honor of Hans-Martin Schenke on the Occasion of the Berliner Arbeitskreis für koptisch-gnostische Schriften's Thirtieth Year*, edited by Hans-Gebhard Bethge et al., 353–74. NHMS 54. Leiden: Brill, 2002.

Foster, Paul. *The Gospel of Peter: Introduction, Critical Edition and Commentary*. TENTS 4. Leiden: Brill, 2010.

Gathercole, Simon. *The Gospel of Judas: Rewriting Early Christianity*. Oxford: Oxford University Press, 2007.

Hedrick, Charles W., and Paul A. Mirecki. *Gospel of the Savior: A New Ancient Gospel*. California Classical Library. Santa Rosa, CA: Polebridge, 1999.

Kasser, Rodolphe, and Gregor Wurst, eds. *The Gospel of Judas Together with the Letter of Peter to Philip, James, and a Book of Allogenes from Codex Tchacos. Critical Edition*. Washington, DC: National Geographic Society, 2007.

Kraus, Thomas J., ed. and trans. "P.Vindob.G 2325: The 'Fayûm Fragment.'" In *Gospel Fragments*, edited by Thomas J. Kraus, et al., 219–27. Oxford Early Christian Gospel Texts. Oxford: Oxford University Press, 2009.

Kraus, Thomas J., and Tobias Nicklas. *Das Petrusevangelium und die Petrusapokalypse: Die griechischen Fragmente mit deutscher und englischer Übersetzung*. Neutestamentliche Apokryphen 1. GCS n.F. 11. Berlin: de Gruyter, 2004.

Layton, Bentley. *The Gnostic Scriptures: A New Translation with Annotations and Introductions*. Garden City, NY: Doubleday, 1987.

Nicklas, Tobias. *Studien zum Petrusevangelium*. WUNT 453. Tübingen: Mohr/Siebeck, 2020.

Plisch, Uwe-Karsten. "Zu einigen Einleitungsfragen des Unbekannten Berliner Evangeliums (UBE)." *ZAC* 9 (2005) 64–84.

Schenke, Hans-Martin. "Das sogenannte 'Unbekannte Berliner Evangelium' (UBE)." *ZAC* 2 (1998) 199–213.

Schmidt, Carl. Review of Jacoby, *Evangelienfragment* in *Göttingische gelehrte Anzeigen* 162 (1900) 481–506.

Suciu, Alin. *The Berlin-Strasbourg Apocryphon: A Coptic Apostolic Memoir*. WUNT 370. Tübingen: Mohr/Siebeck, 2017.

Wayment, Thomas A. "A Reexamination of the Text of P.Oxy. 2949." *JBL* 128 (2009) 375–82.

5

The Teaching of the Risen and Living Jesus

Introduction

IN THREE GOSPELS OF the New Testament, there are reports of appearances of the risen Jesus to his female and male followers. These texts are based on the early Christian confession of the resurrection of Jesus from the dead, which stands at the beginnings of the Christian faith and is connected early on with appearances of the Risen One. The appearance stories present a connection between the earthly activity of Jesus and its continuation under new circumstances in the time after Easter. In the Gospel of Matthew, Jesus appears first to the women as they are walking away from the empty tomb; after this, he appears to his disciples in Galilee and commissions them to make disciples of all nations and to baptize them and instruct them in the teaching of Jesus (Matthew 28:16–20). In the Gospel of Luke, the first appearance story relates to two disciples on the road to Emmaus to whom Jesus appears and with whom he renews the table fellowship from the time of his earthly activity (Luke 24:13–35). After this he appears again to his disciples gathered in Jerusalem, opens to them the understanding of the Scriptures of Israel, which are said to speak of him, and, finally, is taken up into heaven (24:36–53). Acts, which continues the Gospel of Luke, begins with another appearance of Jesus to his disciples. Jesus commissions his disciples to be his witnesses beginning from Jerusalem "to the end of the world" (Acts 1:8). After this, a second ascension of Jesus into heaven is recounted, from where he will return only at the end of time (Acts 1:9–11). In the Gospel of John, Jesus appears first to Mary Magdalene and then to the disciples gathered in Jerusalem. He gives them the Spirit and empowers them to forgive sins. Finally, he appears to Thomas, who initially could not believe the resurrection of the crucified one, and thereby overcomes his doubt (20:1–29). There were apparently no appearances of Jesus in the original version of the Gospel of Mark.

In the appearance stories of the New Testament, the post-resurrection period is set in motion by Jesus himself. It is stressed here that the Risen One is not simply identical to the pre-Easter Jesus. The disciples and Mary Magdalene do not initially recognize him. His appearances are portrayed as theophanies in which he is suddenly present, even in locked rooms, and in which he just as suddenly disappears again. At the same time, it is stressed that in the case of Jesus' appearances we are also not dealing with a spiritual being but, in fact, with the crucified one, who is recognizable through his wounds. This close interweaving of continuity and new beginning is an important feature of the appearance stories of the New Testament.

The appearances of the risen Jesus are a central component of the early Christian Jesus tradition. This is why corresponding narratives were added to the Gospel of Mark after the fact (as 16:9–20). The Gospel of John was also supplemented with a chapter with additional appearances, although a conclusion to the book already appears at the end of chapter 20. The stories of the New Testament Gospels were often taken as a starting point for more extensive reports about the teaching of Jesus as the Risen One. This teaching usually goes far beyond what is in the New Testament and contains traditions that point to developments in the Christianity of the second and third centuries.

Additions to the New Testament Gospels: John 21 and the Secondary Endings of Mark

In the first half of the second century CE, different endings were added to the Gospel of Mark. They recount appearances and instructions of the Risen One to his disciples. The reason for this is that the Gospel of Mark ends in a very odd way—namely, with the note that the women did not carry out the instruction to announce the message of his resurrection to the disciples because they were afraid. The oldest biblical codices from the fourth century CE (Sinaiticus and Vaticanus) end with the statement "for they were afraid" (Mark 16:8). Eusebius, Jerome, and Gregory of Nyssa also know this ending. It is controversial whether the original ending of Mark was lost or whether the narrative did, in fact, end in this peculiar way. In any case, secondary endings are already attested at an early date.

The "shorter ending of Mark" is handed down by Codex Bobiensis, a Latin manuscript from the early fifth century. It says: "And all that had been commanded them they told briefly to those around Peter. And afterward Jesus himself sent out through them, from east to west, the sacred and imperishable proclamation of eternal salvation" (trans. NRSV). Codex Bobiensis correspondingly lacks the statement that the women said nothing to anyone out of fear. Thus, in this manuscript, the Gospel of Mark ends with the carrying out of the instruction of the angel and with Jesus himself being active through the apostles.

The longer ending of Mark, which is also sometimes called the "canonical" ending, appears in numerous manuscripts, with some of the copyists indicating through markings that they were aware that it was added later. This conclusion also appears in today's editions of the Bible, which also usually signal that we are dealing with a supplement that was added later. Some manuscripts even contain both endings. The longer ending of Mark is not designed as a continuation of the Gospel of Mark but arose independently of it. It contains a narrative of multiple appearances, which are dependent on already existing traditions. Jesus appears to Mary Magdalene, to two disciples, and to the eleven disciples (the circle of the twelve without Judas) at a meal. He teaches them about the relationship between faith, baptism, and salvation, and sends them out for the worldwide proclamation of the gospel. Finally, he is taken up into heaven.

A secondary ending was also added to the Gospel of John in the early second century. Unlike the secondary ending of Mark, however, this ending was clearly composed as a continuation of the Gospel of John. While it is closely dependent on the Gospel of John in language and content, it sets different emphases vis-à-vis what comes before. Jesus appears to his disciples at the Sea of Gennesaret (which is called "Sea of Tiberias" in the Gospel of John) and celebrates a meal with them. After this, he establishes Peter as "shepherd" of his "sheep"—i.e., as community leader—with the threefold commission corresponding to Peter's threefold denial. Finally, there is a saying of Jesus about the "Beloved Disciple": If Jesus wishes that he "remains" until Jesus comes, he will remain. This is probably a statement about the continuing significance of this disciple for the community. Finally, in 21:25 we have a second conclusion in addition to the first conclusion found in 20:30–31.

Thus, the subsequently added chapter of the Gospel of John adds another appearance of Jesus and is concentrated on Peter and the Beloved Disciple. In this way, the narrative of the Gospel of John is continued into the situation of the post-resurrection community. The commissioning of Peter indicates that his role is meant to be reinforced, which corresponds to the significance that he has in the Christian tradition.

Thus, the additions to Mark and John show how the appearances of Jesus extend his earthly activity into the post-resurrection period. In this way, what is told about Jesus in the Gospels obtains constitutive meaning for the emerging church. Appearances of the Risen One, however, are also recounted in writings that do not contain accounts of the earthly activity of Jesus before the crucifixion.

The Epistle of the Apostles (*Epistula Apostolorum*)

Although the *Epistula Apostolorum* is an "Epistle of the Apostles" according to the designation that was first given to it in the twentieth century, it belongs to the gospels according to its literary character. The text is completely preserved only in Ethiopic and attested by fourteen manuscripts. These all come from the fifteenth century or later, which points to the enduring significance of the work for the Ethiopian church. Parts of text are also preserved in Coptic and on a single page with Latin text. The work was presumably composed in the second century in Greek—i.e., it belongs to the early gospels outside of the New Testament. According to its narrative framework, it presents itself as a letter of the apostles of Jesus Christ to the churches in the four directions of heaven. It is said to have been written because of the false teaching of Simon and Cerinthus, two names that stand almost paradigmatically for teachings rejected by the church in early Christianity.

The first part (chaps. 1–12) communicates the content of the letter. The apostles, whose names are listed out in chapter 2, testify first to the fact that they heard and touched the Lord Jesus Christ after his resurrection, and that he then revealed astonishing things to them. This is followed by a summary of the activity of Jesus, beginning with the birth through Joseph and Mary, the listing out of miracles of Jesus that are also known from the New Testament Gospels, his crucifixion at the time of

Pontius Pilate and Archelaus (the latter is obviously a chronological error, since Archelaus was only the ruler in Judaea and Samaria until 6 CE), his entombment, and the appearances of the Risen One to three women at the tomb and, finally, to the disciples. This part of the work thus aims to testify to the earthly activity of Jesus, including his death and his appearances after the resurrection.

In chapter 13 a new part begins in which the Risen One gives his disciples instructions about his heavenly existence before he came to earth, his unrecognized arrival in the earthly sphere, and about the resurrection, which concerns flesh, soul, and spirit. The way of Jesus Christ is presented here in a comprehensive form. It begins in the upper world, with the "Father of the all," and leads also to the underworld, to the patriarchs and prophets of Israel. This part is configured as a dialogue between Jesus and his apostles, with the apostles asking questions that serve as starting points for further teachings. This literary form can be found in numerous writings of the second and third centuries, which are, therefore, also called "Dialogue Gospels" or "Appearance Gospels."

In addition to the eleven apostles, Paul also appears in the *Epistula Apostolorum* (31–33). For this, recourse is made to the conversion of Paul in the New Testament book of Acts, which is configured in a distinct way in order to integrate Paul into the circle of the apostles. Jesus prophesies to the apostles that they will encounter Paul, who will be freed from his blindness through their intervention. Jesus then sends the apostles out to proclaim the gospel and commissions them to be "fathers and teachers and servants" of human beings. Finally, Jesus ends the dialogue and announces that the one who sent him will come after three days and three hours in order to take him to himself. This is followed by an account of Jesus' ascension, before the work ends with the saying of Jesus "Go in peace!" (51).

The *Epistula Apostolorum* belongs in a context in which the coming of Jesus Christ "in the flesh"—i.e., his actual incarnation—was just as contested as the bodily resurrection of Christians. There were diverse views about this, including views that were sometimes called "docetic" or "gnostic." What is in mind here are teachings that emphasize the divinity of Jesus and his belonging to the heavenly sphere at the expense of his true humanity. This fundamental problem ultimately affects every presentation in which the divine and human natures of Jesus are meant to be held together. If his divinity is stressed, this can take place at the expense of his humanity, and especially his crucifixion. If, by contrast, his humanity is emphasized, then this raises the question of how one can still speak of his complete divinity. Can it be claimed of a divine being that such a being was executed on the cross and actually died? The problem that surfaces here fundamentally shaped the christological discussion in early Christianity. In the Christian church, the confession was ultimately formulated that Jesus had both a divine and a human nature: "true God from true God," who assumed flesh, was crucified and buried, and rose again on the third day. This formulation from the confession of Nicaea and Constantinople in 381 CE ultimately affirms a paradox or compromise—namely, that in the confession of Jesus Christ, his divinity may not be emphasized at the expense of his humanity, including his passion and death, nor may his humanity be stressed at the expense of his divinity. This confession is the result of difficult controversies that began in the second century and that are also reflected in the *Epistula Apostolorum*. They can also be recognized in a different way in other Appearance Gospels.

The *Gospel of Mary*

The *Gospel of Mary* is primarily attested through a Coptic codex from the fifth century. The manuscript is housed in the Archaeological Center in Berlin as part of the Berlin Papyrus collection with the designation Berolinensis Gnosticus (BG) 8502. It contains four writings, of which two are also found in the codices from Nag Hammadi. The first writing is entitled the *Gospel of Mary*. It is followed by the *Apocryphon of John*, which is attested three times in the Nag Hammadi codices (see below), by the *Wisdom of Jesus Christ*, which is also found in the Nag Hammadi codices (see below), and, finally, by a fourth work titled the *Act of Peter*. Thus, as in the case of Codex Tchacos, there are connections to the Nag Hammadi writings.

Mary is preserved only in an incomplete form in BG 8502. The text begins on page seven. The first six pages are thus lost, as are pages 11 to 14; the text concludes on page 19 with the title *Gospel of Mary* (which is placed at the end, as is often the case in ancient writings). The person in view is evidently Mary Magdalene, who also plays a special role as the first witness of the resurrection in the Gospel of John and appears in other apocryphal gospels.

In addition to the Coptic text from the Berlin Codex, there are also two Greek papyri with fragments of *Mary*. P.Oxy. 3525, which is from the third century, contains a piece of text that is also attested on pages 9–10 of BG 8502. Papyrus Rylands 463, likewise from the third century, offers a Greek parallel to a passage from pages 17–19. Through these papyri, an emergence of the *Gospel of Mary* in Greek is secure for the third and presumably even for the second century.

The preserved text begins in the middle of a dialogue of Jesus with his female and male disciples about matter and salvation (7,1–8,11). The situation of a post-resurrection instruction is apparently presupposed here. Jesus teaches Mary that all things will be dissolved and return to their respective origins. Behind this it is possible to recognize the view that the connection between the upper, spiritual and the lower, material sphere is not permanent; rather, the two will separate from each other again. Matter is evaluated negatively here, because it calls forth unnatural desires. After Jesus has taken leave from them with a greeting of peace and departed, the disciples fall into doubt because they assume that they will not be spared, as Jesus was also not spared. In this situation, Mary rises, kisses the disciples as their sister, and exhorts them not to persist in grief and doubt. After that, Peter exhorts her to tell them the words of the Savior: "Sister, we know that the Savior loved you more than the other women. Tell us the words of the Savior that you remember, which you know and we do not, since we did not hear them" (10,1–6). The fact that Jesus loved Mary the most is also mentioned in the *Gospel of Philip* (on this, see the discussion in chap. 6 below). Here, a competition between Peter and Mary is also recognizable. This is taken up again at the end of the work and intensified.

Mary then recounts the content of the vision, though the beginning is not preserved due to the missing pages (15,1–17,7). It deals with the ascent of the soul, which must pass by four powers that want to hinder it from ascending but cannot do so. The third power—the first one whose name is preserved—is called "Ignorance." The fourth has seven forms. The powers include Desire, Ignorance, and "the Kingdom of the Flesh." The soul is able to destroy everything that seeks to hinder it from ascending and to be saved from the material world.

After the vision, there is an account of a conversation between Andrew and Peter with Mary (17,7–18,21). Andrew and Peter do not believe that the Savior entrusted Mary with the teaching on the ascent of the soul. Peter is even indignant that Mary claims she is more elect than the disciples. At the end, the arbitrating word is spoken by Levi, who reproves Peter for his anger and states that the Savior evidently did, in fact, love Mary "more than us." He exhorts them to put on "the perfect human being" and to proclaim the gospel. The work closes with the note that the disciples set out to do so.

Mary is a witness for an instruction of the risen Jesus about the salvation of the soul through its ascent into the upper world. Here, Jesus' teaching is provided with new content, which differs from his teaching prior to the crucifixion. To this end, *Mary* takes up the situation—which is encountered in the New Testament—of an appearance of the Risen One, who teaches his female and male disciples. As in the *Epistula Apostolorum*, this situation forms the narrative context for new teachings of Jesus. Unlike what we find there, however, the content of *Mary* is oriented not to the corporality of the resurrection but, on the contrary, to the separation of body (matter) and soul. In this we can recognize a controversy that arises in the second century concerning the earthly world, bodily resurrection, and the ascent of the soul. While one side affirms the bodily resurrection of Jesus and of believers, other writings advocate the view—which is oriented to a philosophical (Platonic) position—that salvation only concerns the soul, which must leave the earthly world behind. In *Mary*, this is presented as the content of the vision that Jesus grants only to Mary. The conflict between Mary, on the one hand, and Andrew and Peter, on the other, may also reflect a controversy between different groups in early Christianity, who appealed to different persons from the environment of Jesus as authorities. Mary Magdalene could have appeared as an especially appropriate person for this because she is the first witness of an appearance of Jesus in the Gospel of John and, therefore, could enter into competition with Peter, who became increasingly important in early Christianity.

The Wisdom of Jesus Christ

The *Wisdom of Jesus Christ* is attested by two Coptic manuscripts. It occurs as the fourth writing in Codex III from Nag Hammadi and as the third writing in BG 8502. As in the case of the *Gospel of Thomas* and the *Gospel of Mary*, a fragment has been preserved that attests an emergence of the text in Greek. P.Oxy. 1081, a papyrus page written on both sides from the fourth century, offers a Greek parallel to a dialogue of Jesus with Thomas (this can be deduced from the Coptic parallels) and Mary.

THE TEACHING OF THE RISEN AND LIVING JESUS

A distinctive feature of the work is the fact that it has a close parallel in another writing that does not have a Christian connection. *Eugnostos the Blessed* is a work that is attested by two exemplars in Nag Hammadi (a short and a long version). It contains in epistolary form ("Eugnostos, the blessed, to his own") the same content that Jesus communicates to his female and male disciples in *Wisdom*. The text of *Wisdom* runs parallel for long stretches with that of *Eugnostos the Blessed*. In addition, it contains a narrative frame in which Jesus appears to his twelve disciples and seven female disciples on the "mountain" in Galilee (cf. Matthew 28:16, which mentions the eleven disciples, apart from Judas), which, shortly thereafter, is called the "Mount of Olives" (an inaccurate localization, but one that establishes a connection to the ascension of Jesus). Jesus appears "not in his previous form but in invisible spirit," in the form of a "great angel of light" (91,10–13; trans. Meyer). As in other appearance stories it is thus emphatically stressed that the appearance of the Risen One differed from his previous, earthly existence. This finding permits the conclusion that the teaching reworked in this writing was placed secondarily in the context of a teaching of the Risen One.

The Risen One greets the female and male disciples with a greeting of peace and begins to teach them about "the nature of the universe and the Savior's plan of salvation" (92, 4–5; trans. Meyer). This is followed by more extensive remarks of Jesus—who is usually called "the perfect Savior"—about the nature of God, the upper world, the emergence of the lower world, and the way of salvation. These instructions are repeatedly interrupted by questions from the male and female disciples—Philip, Matthew, Thomas, Bartholomew, and Mary—which further the discussion.

The main content of *Wisdom* is the nature of the upper world. The highest God, who is also called "Forefather," is immortal, unbegotten, unknowable, unreachable, and nameless. This "negative theology" is indeed typical for gnostic writings. It is based in philosophical reflections on God, the world, and human beings, which are taken up from the perspective of Christian theology. Here, salvation is usually presented as knowledge about the upper sphere, which is also regarded as the place of origin and goal of human beings. This mythological idea is often presupposed in dialogues of the Risen One with his female and male disciples and is presented and interpreted in them in different ways. Thereby, the extent to which mythological conceptions are developed or only alluded to can vary, as can the consequences that are drawn from the presented way to salvation. In some writings, the knowledge about the upper world and its relation the earthly realm is the decisive presupposition for salvation, whereas others contain an exhortation to a specific way of life.

As in the *Gospel of Mary*, the knowledge that is necessary for salvation is, in the first instance, what stands at the center in *Wisdom*. This includes the fact that the eternal God has a reflection or likeness, which is called "Father." He is the beginning of all appearances. The beginning of the human being is an immortal, androgynous human being, who is also called "Begetter" and "Self-perfected Mind." His consort is "great Wisdom" (Sophia), with whom he begets the "Son of Man," who is called "Christ" and is, again, an androgynous being. This figure begets the Savior with Wisdom, his consort. Through the fall of Sophia, the lower world came into being, whose creator is called "Yaldabaoth" (this figure also appears in other writings, such as the *Gospel of Judas* and the *Apocryphon of John*), as well as human beings, who are connected through drops of light from the upper world with her. Jesus, as the "perfect Savior," breaks this shackle and enables the ascent of the light to the Father.

Wisdom concludes with the short note that the "blessed Savior," after he had said this, disappeared, and the disciples fell into great joy and began to proclaim the gospel of God, the eternal Father (119,9–16; trans. Meyer).

Wisdom is thus a reinterpretation of the teaching of Jesus based on a myth about the highest God, the emergence of the world, and the salvation of human beings. In this respect, it has points of contact with the *Gospel of Mary*, and these two works probably also appeared in roughly the same period of time. While the teaching about the ascent of the soul is given to Mary in a vision in the *Gospel of Mary*, here it is the Risen One himself who teaches about the highest, good God and the nature of the upper world. In both cases, it is possible to recognize mythological conceptions that place the teaching of Jesus in a different context vis-à-vis the Gospels of the New Testament. Since these Gospels are recognizably presupposed, it is clear that these writings begin with the notion that the decisive content for salvation is first given to the female and male disciples by the risen Jesus.

The *Apocryphon of John*

The *Apocryphon of John* is a work that is fundamental for the post-resurrection dialogues of Jesus. Its significance is already evident from the fact that four Coptic manuscripts of it have been handed down: three from Nag Hammadi—it appears at the beginning of Codices II, III, and IV, which points to its prominence—and one from BG 8502 (here it appears as the second writing after the *Gospel of Mary*). It is necessary to distinguish here between a short version and a long version. The short version appears in NHC III and BG 8502, and the long version in NHC II and IV. Moreover, as with the *Wisdom of Jesus Christ*, another text, which lacks a narrative framework, has close connections with the content of *John*. Irenaeus presents the teaching of the "Barbelo-Gnostics" (or better: "those who know Barbelo") in Book I of *Against Heresies*. This teaching largely agrees with the first part of *John*. Thus, the myth portrayed in the *Apocryphon* was apparently put secondarily into the form of a dialogue of the risen Jesus—here with the disciple John. Irenaeus, who wrote in Greek, obviously knew a Greek version of this teaching, which suggests that the Coptic versions of *John* should be regarded as translations from the Greek. This is also supported by other linguistic observations. Its basic form must have arisen in the second century. The narrative framework can be dated to the third century.

The title of the work is the "Apocryphon of John" (short version) or the "Apocryphon according to John" (long version). The latter can very likely be traced back to a Greek version, as is suggested by the similarity to the construction "Gospel according to ..." in the titles of the New Testament Gospels and other gospels (*Peter, Thomas, Mary*). Thus, *John* clearly understands itself as an "apocryphal" writing that conveys teaching of Jesus that is otherwise hidden. The title is, strictly speaking, incomplete: if translated literally, it would be "The apocryphal ... according to John." The noun to be supplied here is "gospel," analogous to the titles "according to John," "according to Mark," etc., which are likewise incomplete and in accordance with which the title found here was evidently constructed. The connection to John could have been suggested by the fact that Jesus appears in the Gospel of John as the revealer of the heavenly world and salvation and likewise teaches his disciples in rather long farewell discourses (chaps. 14–16).

At the beginning it is recounted that John, the brother of James and son of Zebedee (cf. Mark 1:19), goes to the temple and meets there a

Pharisee named Arimanias (or Arimanios). This Pharisee objects that the teacher whom John follows has deceived them and turned them away from the traditions of their fathers. As in P.Oxy. 840 (see above), the Pharisee plays the role of the person who emphasizes the significance of the Jewish traditions, whereas Jesus is distanced from them. John does not answer but becomes sad and asks aloud about the origin of the Savior and the nature of the aeon "to which we will go." With this he specifies the questions that often play a fundamental role in gnostic writings and are at the same time the basic questions of philosophy: Where do we come from? Where are we going? What should we do? What path leads to salvation? (II 1,21–29).

While John ponders this, he receives a luminous vision in which Christ appears to him as a child, then shortly thereafter as an old man, then in many other forms. He introduces himself to John as "I am the [Father.] I am the Mother. I am the Son. I am the undefiled and uncontaminated One" (II 2,12–16; trans. Waldstein/Wisse). He tells John that he will teach him "about what is and [what was] into being and what will come to pass, that you [may know] the things which are not manifest [and the things which are] manifest and to teach you concerning the perfect [Man]" (II 2,16–20; trans. Waldstein/Wisse).

This is followed by the myth that also appears in Irenaeus and that can be designated as the "basic myth" of Gnosticism (see the discussion of the *Gospel of Judas* in chap. 4 above). It begins with a detailed portrayal of the upper God, who exists invisibly and incorruptibly as pure light and is the origin of everything (see also the "negative theology" in the *Wisdom of Jesus Christ*). An important feature of the myth is the orientation to an unknowable origin that is infinitely far away from the world. Right at the beginning of his teaching to John, the Savior introduces the invisible, eternal, and immeasurable One in an extensive way:

> It is not right to think of him as a god or something similar for he is more than a god. (He is) a rule over which nothing rules, for there is nothing before him. Nor does he need them. He does not need life, for he is eternal. He does not need anything, for he cannot be perfected, as if he were lacking and thus needing to be perfected; rather he is always completely perfect. He is light. He is illimitable since there is no one prior to him to set limits to him, the unsearchable One since there exists no one prior to him to examine him, the immeasurable One since no one else

measured him ... the invisible One since no one saw him ..." (II 2,33–3,13; trans. Waldstein/Wisse)

Barbelo, as the feminine principle, appears alongside the eternal, unknowable God. She arises as the manifestation of the thought of the unlimited God—i.e., she is completely related to him:

> And his thought became actual and she came forth and attended him in the brilliance of the light. She is the power who is before the All, who came forth. She is the perfect Providence of the All, the light, the image, the invisible One, the perfect power, Barbelo, the perfect aeon of glory ... And she knows him. She is the first Thought, his image. (II 4,37–5,6; trans. Waldstein/Wisse)

In the development of the myth of the upper world diverse emanations are introduced, such as Providence (Forethought), Aphtharsia (Indestructibility), *Zôê* (Eternal Life), and *Alêtheia* (Truth). The only-begotten One, who is also called *Autogenês* ("the divine Self-Generated"), "the first-born Son of the All of the Spirit," and who is anointed by the invisible Spirit, emerges from the begetting of a spark of light in Barbelo and Reason is granted to him as his fellow worker.

Another specific feature of the myth, which also appears in other writings, are the "four great lights." They come forth from the Light, which is Christ, and the Indestructibility; they symbolize Grace, Understanding, Perception, and Prudence, with each of them having three additional aeons that belong to them (II 7,30–8,20). In this context are introduced "the perfect true Man" who is named Adam, and his son Seth, "who is set over the second light Oroiael" (II 8,28–9,14; trans. Waldstein/Wisse).

The negative part of the myth begins with the presentation of Sophia (Wisdom). She wants to bring forth a likeness out of herself, but, since she acts without the collaboration of the Spirit, she brings forth Yaldabaoth. When she realizes what she has done, she hides and casts him away. Yaldabaoth himself brings forth twelve powers (archons) and installs seven kings, through which he exercises power over the lower world. He is "a jealous God," who says of himself that "there is no other God besides me." Yaldabaoth is thus stylized as a negative caricature of the Old Testament God. He copulates with "Arrogance" and begets twelve angels and commands that seven kings should rule (II 9,26–12,33).

The cosmology is followed by a portrayal of the creation of human beings. The "archon" Yaldabaoth says, "Let us create the human being in the image of God and in our likeness" (II 15,2–4; trans. Waldstein/

Wisse)—a clear allusion to the story of the creation of the human being in Genesis. In the long version, this creation is then portrayed in detail as a collaborative work to which all the archons contribute something. Yaldabaoth, who, due to his origin, has life-giving spirit in himself, breaths something of this into the human being (Adam) (II 19, 25–33). The reinterpretation of the biblical creation story begun here is continued in what follows (19,34–24,8). The earthly rulers are jealous and bring Adam into paradise, where he is to eat from the tree of knowledge. At this point John asks whether it was not the snake who taught Adam this, but the Savior responds that the snake learned to eat "from the evil of begetting." There is then a narration of the creation of the woman (Eve) in the image of the companion that was already given to Adam earlier and was named *Zôê*. Yaldabaoth curses Adam and Eve and casts them out of paradise. He then rapes Eve, which results in the birth of Eloim and Jave (two Old Testament designations for God), who, respectively have a bear-face and a cat-face; the two sons of Eve correspond to Cain and Abel. Adam, however, begets with Eve a child of his own likeness and names him Seth (II 24,35–25,2).

At this point, a dialogue between John and the Savior is inserted, which deals with the salvation of the souls (II 25,16–27,30). The souls upon which the Spirit of life descends will be saved, whereas the others will be brought to the place of eternal punishment.

Yaldabaoth regrets that he made human beings at all and wants to destroy them through a flood (II 28, 32–30,11). *Noë* (an allusion to Noah) is informed of this through *Pronoia* (Forethought) and he hides himself with many people from the "unshakeable race," so that they do not perish. It is explicitly stated that they did not hide themselves in an ark but in a cloud of light—another explicit reinterpretation of the biblical story. After this, angels sent by Yaldabaoth beget with earthly women descendants who die without knowing the truth (cf. Genesis 6:1–4). Finally, *Pronoia*, who appears as a first-person narrator in the concluding section, enters into the earthly sphere of darkness, brings recollection to the human being, and raises him up, so that death no longer has power over him (II 30,12–31,31).

After this, the framework story is taken up again. John is told to write down what he has heard, keep it, and under no circumstances—for example, not in return for a gift—should he pass it on. The Savior disappears again, and John goes to his fellow disciples in order to proclaim to them what he has heard (II 31,21–32,5).

The *Apocryphon of John* thus contains a developed myth about the upper world, the emergence of the lower world, and the creation of the human being. As in other writings from Nag Hammadi (such as the *Hypostasis of the Archons* and *On the Origin of the World*), this myth is a polemical reinterpretation of the biblical creation story from Genesis 1–7 with the help of Platonic motifs. Behind this, we can discern an interest in developing an alternative to the Israelite-Jewish conception of God and salvation as a context for the Christian faith. This interest is also recognizable in other "Dialogue Gospels" (such as the *Gospel of Mary* and the *Wisdom of Jesus Christ*, discussed above), though it is not configured there as a provocative rejection of biblical content. Of the apocryphal gospels, the *Apocryphon of John* is the writing that most extensively connects a gnostic myth of creation and redemption to a narrative frame and thereby presents it as a teaching of the Savior Jesus.

The *Apocryphon of James*

The *Apocryphon of James* is attested in a Coptic version as the second writing in NHC I. Like other writings of this genre, it presumably comes from the second century. While the work has an epistolary framework (as does the previously discussed *Epistula Apostolorum*, to which *James* shows some connections), it is, according to its content, a dialogue of the risen Jesus with his disciples.

In the epistolary framework, James (the brother of Jesus and the son of Zebedee are apparently identified with each other here) writes to a person whose name is not completely preserved, in order to communicate to him a teaching that is characterized as "apocryphal":

> [James] writes to [. . .]thos: Peace [be with you from] Peace, [love from] Love . . . Since you asked that I send you a secret book which was revealed to me and Peter by the Lord, I could not turn you away or gainsay (?) you; but [I have written] it in the Hebrew alphabet and sent it to you, and you alone. (1,1–18; trans. Williams)

The letters "-thos" in the address can perhaps be amended to "Kerinthos," whom Irenaeus opposed as a heretic. Moreover, as in the *Gospel of Judas*, the *Apocryphon of John*, and the *Gospel of Thomas*, the content is explicitly characterized as "secret," in order to distinguish it from other teachings. Here, what is in view is presumably the teachings of Jesus found in the New Testament Gospels, which are supplemented and surpassed by a further-reaching instruction that is not openly accessible.

Another narrative framework begins with the appearance of Jesus, the Savior, 550 days after his resurrection, to the twelve disciples who are sitting together and reminiscing about what the Savior had said to them, "whether in secret or openly, and [putting it …] in books" (2,1–15). The Savior announces that he will go to the place from which he came. The situation is thus comparable to what we find in the other Dialogue Gospels. Jesus then calls to himself James and Peter from the circle of the disciples in order "to fill" them—i.e., to communicate special revelations to them (2,29–39). This is followed by a conversation between Jesus and James and Peter, which represents the main content of the work.

James appears here as the narrator and main conversation partner of Jesus, whereas Peter is more of a marginal figure. The scene has analogies to several previously discussed writings (*Gospel of Mary, Wisdom of Jesus Christ, Apocryphon of John*), but it is especially reminiscent of the *Gospel of Judas*, where Judas is called out of the circle of the twelve disciples in order to receive special revelations. As there, the disciples are also presented as uncomprehending. This becomes clear both in the devaluation of what the disciples wrote down as recollections—presumably a polemic against the New Testament Gospels as "reminiscences of the apostles" (as Justin calls them)—and again at the end when the disciples become angry over what Peter and James communicate to them. The disciples ask James and Peter:

> "What did you hear from the Master? And what has he said to you? And where did he go?" But we answered them, "He has ascended and has given us a pledge and promised life to us all and revealed to us children (?) who are to come after us, after bidding [us] love them, as we would be [saved] for their sakes." And when they heard (this), they indeed believed the revelation, but were displeased about those to be born. And so, not wishing to give them offense, I sent each one to another place. But I myself went up to Jerusalem, praying that I might obtain a portion among the beloved, who will be made manifest. (15,30–16,11; trans. Williams)

At the beginning of the Savior's teaching to James and Peter, those who have (only) seen the Son of Man are cursed, whereas those who have not seen him and not spoken to him are blessed. This is a reference to the episode in John 20, where Jesus blesses those who have not seen and yet

THE TEACHING OF THE RISEN AND LIVING JESUS

have come to believe (John 20:29). In this way, the *Apocryphon of James* relates the teaching of the Savior to the time after his resurrection and departure.

The content of Jesus' revelations is the path to salvation through knowledge and following the words of Jesus. This includes adherence to Jesus, which means discipleship to the point of suffering. In response to James's objection, "Lord, do not mention to us the cross and death, for they are far from you," Jesus answers, "Verily I say unto you, none will be saved unless they believe in my cross. But those who have believed in my cross, theirs is the kingdom of God. Therefore, become seekers for death, like the dead who seek for life; for that which they seek is revealed to them" (5,36–6,10; trans. Williams). Jesus also refers to the violent death of John the Baptist: "Do you not know that the head of prophecy was cut off with John?" (6,29–30; trans. Williams).

Thus, the way into the kingdom of God leads through suffering, which Jesus had previously proclaimed in parables but now pronounces openly. The teaching of Jesus about the kingdom of God is presented as a seed parable in the three aspects of faith, love, and works. The person who has sown the seed of wheat—the logos (teaching)—trusts it. After it has grown, he loves it. When the harvest is completed, he is saved, because he has processed it for nourishment (7,23–35).

There are numerous connections to the sayings and parables from earlier Gospels and Jesus traditions—for example, in the description of discipleship as leaving family and home and in the allusions to the parables of the sower (Mark 4), of the lamps of the virgins (Matthew 25), and of the lost coin (Luke 15). However, these allusion are not presented as explicit quotations. The reason for this is presumably that the earlier Gospels are regarded as inadequate, and another "secret" teaching, which provides a fresh interpretation for earlier Jesus traditions, is set over against them. This is done, however, in a much less polemical way than in the *Gospel of Judas* or the *Apocryphon of James*. And there is also no developed mythology about the upper world and an inferior creator god. However, we do find the notion of the salvation of the Spirit, which opposes the attachment to the earthly world and will be obtained through "children who come after us" (15,38).

The *Dialogue of the Savior*

The *Dialogue of the Savior* is found in a fragmentarily preserved Coptic manuscript designated NHC III. Its origin can be placed in the second or third century. As in the previously discussed works, we are dealing with a dialogue of the risen Jesus, here with Matthew, Judas, and Mary. Here "Dialogue" is even the title of the writing. This is to be taken very literally, since it begins immediately with a speech of the Savior and also ends with one—i.e., it does not have a narrative frame.

The work begins with the following statement of the Savior (who is also often called "the Lord" in this writing): "Now the time has come, brothers and sisters, for us to leave our labor behind and stand at rest" (120,1–6; trans. Meyer). The term *anapausis* ("rest") is used in quite a few gnostic writings to designate the place of salvation. Then follows a conversation in which Matthew, Judas, and Mary ask Jesus questions and thus provide him with the opportunity to develop the teaching about salvation. The concern here is with the knowledge of the path to salvation, which also includes knowledge about the origin of the world. This knowledge is developed in the form of a short creation myth that depends on the biblical creation narrative: Before heaven and earth arose, darkness and water and spirit were over the water; evil entered in order to destroy true understanding; the Father sent the Logos into the world, who brought good gifts to the earth, in order that it might have no lack (127, 22–130,22). Both here and in other passages, the *Dialogue of the Savior* shows a closeness to the Gospel of John. The Lord teaches them that one cannot see the place of life as long as one wears flesh. However, Jesus reveals to the three disciples the high place and the place of the abyss—i.e., the places of salvation and punishment. The archons currently rule over human beings, but those who belong to the Lord will rule in the future. At present they are still in the place of lack, but in the future they will be in the fullness from which they come. The "works of the female" will be abolished there—a motif that sometimes occurs in gnostic writings and that corresponds to the notion of the original, androgynous unity of the human being, which is to be attained again when the female becomes male (see the discussion of the *Gospel of the Egyptians* in chap. 3 above; this motif is also found at the end of the *Gospel of Thomas*). At the end, the Savior exhorts them to overcome anger and envy, in order to obtain rest and eternal life. In doing so, one must ensure that spirits and souls are not led astray (146,18—147,22).

The *Gospel of Thomas*

The *Gospel of Thomas* is perhaps the most famous apocryphal gospel. It was discovered in 1945 in the context of the findings at Nag Hammadi. There it is the second writing in Codex II, after the *Apocryphon of John*. The Coptic manuscript from Nag Hammadi is also the only nearly complete text of *Thomas*. However, around the turn from the nineteenth to the twentieth century, Greek papyri with sayings of Jesus were discovered by Grenfell and Hunt at Oxyrhynchus— namely, the papyri with the numbers 1, 654, and 655. Papyrus 1 contains Greek parallels to sayings 26 to 30 in the Coptic text. Papyrus 654 contains the (fragmentary) beginning of the gospel with the introduction: "These are the secret sayings that the living Jesus spoke . . . ," as well as parallels to sayings 1 to 7. Finally, Papyrus 655 contains a dialogue between Jesus and his disciples that has points of contact with sayings 36 and 37 of the Coptic text. However, Papyrus 655 deviates clearly from the Coptic text in both content and literary character. It is especially striking that this Papyrus lacks the characteristic structure of the sayings of Jesus in *Thomas*, which usually introduces the sayings with "Jesus says." Accordingly, without knowledge of the Coptic manuscript, Grenfell and Hunt had given Papyrus 1 and Papyrus 654 the designations "Logia of Jesus" or "New Sayings of Jesus," whereas they published Papyrus 655 under the heading "Fragment of a Lost Gospel." Whether Papyrus 655 comes from a Greek version of *Thomas* (which deviated significantly from the Coptic text) or whether it belongs to an otherwise unknown gospel that was reworked in *Thomas* must remain an open question.

The Greek papyri, which come from different manuscripts dated from the beginning or middle of the third century, as well as the Coptic manuscript from Nag Hammadi, point to the fact that *Thomas* was probably composed in Greek in the second century and was disseminated to some extent. Very soon, however, it was rejected as "heretical" by Christian theologians; prior to the discovery at Nag Hammadi, it was known to us only through a few references in ancient authors. Since the discovery of the Nag Hammadi codices, however, *Thomas* has become one of the most discussed apocryphal gospels and gained great importance for the interpretation of the person and teaching of Jesus in ancient Christianity.

The immense interest in the writing is reflected in editions and translations of the text in numerous languages and in many commentaries and individual studies on various aspects of the work. In particular, there has been a focus on the relationship between *Thomas* and the New Testament Gospels, and especially to the Synoptic Gospels. This is an obvious comparison, since about half of the sayings of *Thomas* have parallels in the Synoptic Gospels, and there are also some analogies to the presentation of Jesus in the Gospel of John. Some of the common sayings are assigned to the oldest stock of the Jesus tradition, so *Thomas* could lead us back to the beginnings of the Jesus tradition. This hypothesis is supported by the fact that quite a few of the sayings and parables of Jesus in *Thomas* do not appear to be directly dependent on the New Testament Gospels. Moreover, it is hypothesized that *Thomas* could belong to the beginnings of the Jesus tradition based on its literary genre as a collection of sayings and parables. The Sayings Source Q, an early collection of sayings and speeches of Jesus inferred to have been used as a source by Matthew and Luke, has been pointed to as an analog, with the implication that collections of sayings may have preceded the composition of narrative gospels.

However, it has also been repeatedly stressed that *Thomas* exhibits quite a few features that separate it from the New Testament Gospels and point to a second-century milieu. This includes above all the emphasis on the knowledge that is needed for salvation and is mediated through Jesus. Moreover, in quite a few sayings we find terms and notions that can scarcely be associated with the beginnings of the Jesus tradition in the first century, such as the talk of an image of the human being and its likeness (saying 84), which appears to presuppose the Platonic model of a heavenly original and its earthly copy, or the term "bridal chamber" (saying 104).

For this reason, a very heated, controversial debate has developed over *Thomas* and its usefulness in reconstructing the history of the early Jesus tradition. Recent scholarship argues that the writing must first be understood according to its own literary and thematic characteristics, and thus be placed in the history of early Christianity. Only on this basis can the relationship to the New Testament Gospels be determined. Moreover, it has been pointed out that on its own the literary character of a sayings source is not an indicator for assigning an early date to the writing. In addition, the analogy to the Sayings Source Q—which, for its part, is a scholarly hypothesis and not a text—is not particularly convincing. In the case of Q we are evidently dealing with an early collection of Jesus traditions that included sayings and speeches of Jesus as well as some narrative material that approaches biographically-oriented narratives as we have them in the Synoptic Gospels. This collection, whose scope and literary form cannot be determined more exactly, represents a preliminary stage of the narrative Gospels and could, therefore, also be integrated into them. *Thomas*, by contrast, is an entirely different case. Although it may contain sayings and parables that can be traced back to the earliest strata of the Jesus tradition, earlier gospels are presupposed and were used in order to extract sayings and parables of Jesus from them. In Thomas, these earlier traditions are organized in a new way, and are introduced in each case with "Jesus says." Thus, regardless of the origin of the traditions themselves, the framework and concept of *Thomas* are from a later time. The closest literary analogies are not the hypothetical Sayings Source Q, but the Jewish "Sayings of the Fathers" or collections such as the *Sentences of Sextus* or Epicurus's *Principle Doctrines*, which is attached to the presentation of his activity in Diogenes Laertius's work *Lives and Opinions of Eminent Philosophers*.

At the beginning of *Thomas* we find a statement about the content, which also functions as a reading guide:

> These are the hidden sayings that the living Jesus spoke and Didymus Judas Thomas wrote down. And he said, "Whoever finds the interpretation of these sayings will not taste death." (saying 1)

Here, the sayings of Jesus are characterized as "secret" (or "hidden")—i.e., as teaching that is not openly accessible. They have been spoken by the "living" Jesus. This leaves open whether the teachings of Jesus from the time of his earthly activity are in view or whether the concern is with teachings of the Risen One. This distinction is not important for *Thomas* and, therefore, may perhaps be consciously left open. Some episodes recounted in what follows clearly look back to Jesus' earthly activity. For example, there are reports of conversations with the male and female disciples (e.g., sayings 6, 12, 13, 18, 20, 79, etc.), which appear to presuppose situations in the earthly activity of Jesus. This is also the case when an observation of Jesus or the disciples becomes the occasion for a teaching (e.g., sayings 22, 60, 99). Saying 28 ("Jesus said, 'I stood in the midst of the world and appeared to them in flesh'") probably also looks back to the earthly activity of Jesus.

Many sayings and parables are introduced without a specific narrative situation with "Jesus says." The Coptic verb can be translated as present ("Jesus says") or as past ("Jesus said"). The literary character of

Thomas as well as the parallels to the Greek fragments, where a present form is clearly recognizable at some points (though this could also be interpreted as a "historical present," i.e., as a past-tense form) indicate, however, that *Thomas* presents the sayings of Jesus as teachings that have enduring significance. Jesus speaks directly to the readers or hearers in his sayings and parables, for which reason the translation "Jesus says" is indeed appropriate in most cases. The text's principle concern is with the teaching of Jesus as the way to salvation. Accordingly, the passion, death, and resurrection of Jesus play no role in *Thomas*. Finally, in the introduction, "Didymus Judas Thomas" is specified as the one who has written down the sayings of Jesus. Within the writing, Thomas then appears once more. In saying 13 Jesus entrusts three words to Thomas that he does not pass on to his fellow disciples because they would stone him if he did. Thus, the disciple Thomas plays a prominent role in *Thomas*, a role that can be compared to the role of Mary in the *Gospel of Mary* and of Judas in the *Gospel of Judas*. His name could also point to this specific role. "Didymus" is the Greek and "Thomas" the Aramaic term for "twin." Thus, Thomas could be given the role of the "twin"—i.e., of the one who has become like Jesus—which is regarded as the goal of understanding the sayings of Jesus in the gospel.

In the introduction, there is then an exhortation to seek the meaning of the sayings of Jesus, which leads to eternal life. This is then immediately taken up again in saying 2:

> Jesus said, "The one who seeks should not cease seeking until he finds. And when he finds he will be disturbed; and when he is disturbed, he will marvel. And he will rule over the all."

As already noted, this saying is known to Clement of Alexandria, who ascribes it to the *Gospel according to the Hebrews*. It could be used in different contexts in order to point to the importance of the proper understanding of the teaching of Jesus. It need not be a "gnostic" motif in the sense of a teaching based on a specific myth. Knowledge as the way that leads to the goal of human life—i.e., to its perfection, redemption, or to the overcoming of its attachment to the earthly, material world—is a widespread philosophical *topos* that has also found its way into the Jesus tradition.

In *Thomas*, this saying points to what is important in the teaching of Jesus. The concern is with recognizing where humans come from and where they are going. Accordingly, Jesus says in saying 50: "If they say to you, 'Where have you come from?' tell them 'We have come from the light, from the place where the light came to be on its own, established itself, and was revealed in their image.'" Saying 49 is closely related to this: "Blessed are the solitary ones and the elect, for you will find the kingdom. For you have come from it and you will return there." Thus, Jesus teaches his disciples that they come from the "kingdom" (which is elsewhere called the "kingdom of the Father") and will also return there. The mention of "solitary ones" and "elect" is connected with this. A communal life does not come into view in *Thomas*. A community ethic is not developed, and rituals, including the common meal, are not mentioned. Instead, the readers are addressed as individual elect persons, who should strive for insight into the meaning of the sayings of Jesus (thus also in sayings 4, 15, 22, 23, and 75).

Accordingly, the ethos of *Thomas* is oriented to the individual disciple of Jesus. This ethos can be characterized as radical and ascetic. The addressees are exhorted to "renounce the world" (110; cf. also saying 27). Indeed, the world is even designated as a "corpse" (56). Saying 42— "Become passersby"—could also belong here, for it could describe the attitude toward the world that the disciples of Jesus are meant to cultivate. This includes the renunciation of possessions, care for those who are persecuted and hungry, and the loaning of money without demanding it back. The disciples is to love one's brother as one's own life and protect the brother as the apple of one's eye (saying 25).

Critical controversy with Jewish traditions occurs frequently in the text. Circumcision is not useful; if it were, it would belong to the nature of the human being (saying 53). The Sabbath should not be kept on one day of the week; rather, one should abstain from the world for the whole week (27). The Jewish rituals of almsgiving, prayer, and fasting are judged negatively and excluded as practices for the disciples of Jesus (6 and 13). These harsh allusions to Jewish traditions are not necessarily to be regarded as reflections of an actual controversy of *Thomas* with Judaism. Such an interpretation appears unlikely in view of the fact that Jesus' words are presented as a philosophical teaching on the way back to the origin of humanity. The recourse to Jewish traditions can be better understood as an interpretation of the activity of Jesus that is critical of cultic-ritual practices and instead promotes a radical ethos of denying the world and turning to the poor and the persecuted. A criticism of the interpretation of the teaching of Jesus in the context of Jewish writings and traditions could stand behind this. *Thomas* is oriented instead to a philosophical-ethical instruction of the individual disciple of Jesus, which aims at the perfection of the human being through insight into the origin and goal of his life and the consequences that follow from this for one's conduct.

Sources and Studies

Boer, Esther de. *The Gospel of Mary: Beyond a Gnostic and a Biblical Mary Magdalene.* JSNTSup 260. London: T. & T. Clark, 2004.
DeConick, April D. *The Original Gospel of Thomas in Translation: With a Commentary and New English Translation of the Complete Gospel.* LNTS 287. London: T. & T. Clark, 2007.
Gathercole, Simon J. *The Composition of the Gospel of Thomas: Original Language and Influences.* SNTSMS 151. Cambridge: Cambridge University Press, 2012.
Grenfell, Bernard P., and Arthur S. Hunt, eds. *The Oxyrhynchus Papyri.* London: Egypt Exploration Fund, 1898–1904 (vol. 1 for P.Oxy. 1; vol. 4 for P. Oxy. 654 and 655).
Hartenstein, Judith, and Silke Petersen. "Gospel of Mary: Mary Magdalene as Beloved Disciple and Representative of Jesus." In *Feminist Biblical Interpretation: A Compendium of Critical Commentary on the Books of the Bible and Related Literature,* edited by Luise Schottroff and Marie-Theres Wacker, 943–56. Grand Rapids: Eerdmans, 2012.
Hills, Julian V. *The Epistle of the Apostles.* Early Christian Apocrypha 2. Santa Rosa, CA: Polebridge, 2009.
King, Karen L. *The Gospel of Mary of Magdala: Jesus and the First Woman Apostle.* Santa Rosa, CA: Polebridge, 2003.
Layton, Bentley. *Nag Hammadi Codex II, 2–7, together with XIII, 2* Brit. Lib. Or. 4926(1) and P. Oxy. 1, 654, 655.* NHS 20. Leiden: Brill, 1989.
Meyer, Marvin, ed. *The Nag Hammadi Scriptures. The Revised and Updated Translation of Sacred Gnostic Texts, Complete in One Volume.* New York: HarperOne, 2007 ("Wisdom of Jesus Christ," 287–96; "Dialogue of the Savior," 301–11).
Plisch, Uwe-Karsten. *The Gospel of Thomas: Original Text with Commentary.* Translated by Gesine Schenke Robinson. Stuttgart: Deutsche Bibelgesellschaft, 2009.
Shoemaker, Stephen J. "A Case of Mistaken Identity? Naming the Gnostic Mary." In *Which Mary? The Marys of Early Christian Tradition,* edited by F. Stanley Jones, 5–30. SBLSymS 19. Atlanta: Society of Biblical Literature, 2003.
Tuckett, Christopher. *The Gospel of Mary.* Oxford Early Christian Gospel Texts. Oxford: Oxford University Press, 2007.
Waldstein, Michael, and Frederik Wisse. *The Apocryphon of John: Synopsis of Nag Hammadi Codices II,1; III,1; and IV,1 with BG 8502,2.* NHMS 33. Leiden: Brill, 1995.
Watson, Francis. *An Apostolic Gospel: "The Epistula Apostolorum" in Literary Context.* SNTSMS 179. Cambridge: Cambridge University Press, 2021.
Williams, Francis E. "The Apocryphon of James. Introduction, Text and Translation." In *Nag Hammadi Codex I (The Jung Codex),* vol. 1, edited by Harold W. Attridge, 13–53. 2 vols. NHS 22–23. Leiden: Brill, 1985.

6

Other Gospels

The *Gospel of Philip*

THE *GOSPEL OF PHILIP* comes right after the *Gospel of Thomas* in Codex II from Nag Hammadi. It is possible that this reflects the intention to have two writings that are explicitly characterized as "gospel" in their titles (which stand at the end of these two writings) appear in succession. Moreover, the two writings are formally comparable in the fact that they are largely composed of unconnected sayings or episodes that are strung together. At the same time, *Philip* differs clearly from the *Gospel of Thomas* in form and content. Here, Jesus is only rarely the speaker of sayings and also appears only occasionally as an agent. Instead, there is often reflection *about* Jesus—about the meaning of his name, about his appearance, about his origin, and about his coming into the world. Thus, *Philip* is not a collection of sayings or a "Sayings Gospel," even though this designation is sometimes applied to it. Rather, *Philip* contains loosely connected philosophical or mythological reflections that can be designated as "aphorisms," which give the writing a quite distinctive character. It can be designated, therefore, as a "philosophical gospel," with it being clear that "gospel" must be understood in a quite different way here—i.e., in comparison to what is the case for the Gospels of the New Testament, the *Gospel of Peter*, the *Gospel of Mary*, and the *Gospel of Thomas*.

A gospel that bears the name Philip—the name was presumably attached to the writing secondarily because Philip is the only apostle mentioned in the writing (91)—is referenced in the fourth century by

Epiphanius, who quotes a passage from it (*Pan.* 26.13). While this quotation does not appear in *Philip*, it does have thematic points of contact with it. Accordingly, Epiphanius could have known a different version of the work—which is indeed possible, since different manuscripts could deviate from one another, especially in the case of works that have the character of collections. Thus, a "Gospel according to Philip" would have had to exist in the fourth century at the latest. It is conceivable, however, that the writing already arose in the second or third century. As with other writings, with *Philip* we are dealing with an originally Greek work that was translated into Coptic.

Philip belongs to a strand of ancient Gnosticism that is called "Valentinian Gnosticism" after its founder and first teacher Valentinus, who was active in Rome around the middle of the second century. It represents a somewhat different form of gnostic system than what we find in the *Gospel of Judas* and the *Apocryphon of John*, which were introduced above. The Valentinian system knows a highest God, who is called *Bythos* (Greek for "Depth"). There comes alongside him, as a feminine principle, *Ennoia* (Thought) or *Sigê* (Silence). Additional emanations follow, which lead to a strictly structured system in which in the upper aeon *Nous* (Understanding) and *Alêtheia* (Truth), *Logos* (Word) and *Zôê* (Life), as well as *Anthrôpos* (Human Being) and *Ecclêsia* (Community) are coordinated to one another in pairs. Further emanations are located on lower aeons. At the lower end is Sophia (Wisdom), through whose fall the world brought forth by the demiurge arose. Within this system, Christ and the Holy Spirit also have their place. According to Valentinian teaching, the human being consists of *pneuma* (spirit) and *sôma* (body). The human being is connected to the upper sphere through their *pneuma*, though this is imprisoned in the material world. Salvation consists in a process of understanding through which human beings perceive that they are connected to the divine sphere, but must leave soul and body behind them in order to get there.

The Valentinian system is described in detail by Irenaeus in his work *Against Heresies* and—from his perspective—refuted. At the time of Irenaeus, Valentinianism was apparently a very popular philosophical and theological teaching. And there were still Valentinians for multiple centuries in and on the margins of the church. In the Valentinian texts there are prayers and other liturgical texts that point to a religious and communal practice, and sacraments also play an important role. This can also be recognized in *Philip* .

The abundance of themes and reflections that are found in *Philip* can be illustrated here only through a limited selection. In *Philip* 13 we read:

> The archons wanted to deceive man, since they saw that he had a kinship with the truly good. They took the name of the good and gave it to what is not good, in order (first) to deceive him through the names and bind them to what is not good, and then, as if they were doing them a favor, to cause them to remove from the 'not good' and transfer them to the 'good' which they think is so. For they wished to take the free man and make him their slave forever. (trans. Schenke)

In *Philip* and in many other texts, the "archons" are evil powers that seek to hinder the salvation of humans—i.e., their liberation from the earthly world. A deception is depicted in the text. The archons delude the original human into thinking that what is actually bad is good in order to bind him to the world and make him into a "slave." Section 21 says:

> Those who say that the Lord first died and then rose up are in error. For he rose up first and then died. If anyone does not first attain the resurrection, he will not (be able to) die. As God lives, that one would [die]. (trans. Schenke)

In this aphorism the sequence of life and death is turned into its opposite in a paradoxical way. "Life" is understood as the true life that is determined by the resurrection and, therefore, leads to salvation and is distinguished from earthly, physical life. Because Jesus has "brought on this true 'life,'" he rose first and then died a physical death. Here, an echo of the talk of "life" in the Gospel of John can be recognized. Right at the beginning, John says regarding the Logos that "life" was in him (John 1:4), and Jesus says concerning himself: "I am the resurrection and the life" (11:25; cf. 14:6). In *Philip* too, we encounter such a specifically defined talk of "life." It says that during one's earthly life, a person must obtain a share in the resurrection life mediated by Jesus. After this, one will die a physical death but already has in oneself the life that reaches beyond that death. In section 63c of *Philip*, it says in an analogous way that it befits us (human beings), as long as we are in the world, to attain the resurrection, so that when we divest ourselves of the flesh, we may attain (to the place of) rest.

In section 23, this theme is connected to the Eucharist as the sacrament through which one gains a share in the life of Jesus. The talk of "resurrection" and "likeness" in section 67 can be connected with this. The passage begins with the explanation that the truth came into the world "in types and images." This is then related to rebirth and resurrection, which occur through the likeness. As in the *Gospel of Thomas*, this is based on the notion of archetype or original and likeness or copy, with the goal of the human being lying in the union with the archetype through the resurrection or in becoming one with Jesus.

In section 68, the sacraments are mentioned: "The Lord [did] everything in a mystery: baptism, chrism, eucharist, redemption and bridal chamber." The five Valentinian sacraments are possibly to be understood as a climax. In that case, the "bridal chamber" would be the completed union of the believers with the divine sphere. It is more likely, however, that "salvation" and "bridal chamber" represent interpretations of the three previously mentioned sacraments. The rituals of baptism, anointing, and eucharist lead to salvation, which is presented as union in the bridal chamber (cf. 61a, 76, 79, 82). In any case, the passage is an attestation for the meaning of the sacraments, which also appear at other points. Thus, there is frequent talk of baptism, anointing, and Eucharist, and it is possible to recognize an intensification within these rituals. Anointing is superior to baptism (95a). The Eucharist is the ritual through which the union with Jesus occurs (23; cf. 100: "When we drink this (cup) [i.e., the blood of the perfect man], we shall receive for ourselves the perfect man").

As in the *Gospel of Mary*, Mary Magdalene plays a prominent role in *Philip*. Section 55b says:

> The S[avior lov]ed [Ma]ry Mag[da]lene more than [all] the disciples, and kissed her on her [mouth] often. The other [disciples . . .]. They said to him: "Why do you love her more than all of us?" The Savior answered and said to them: "Why do I not love you like her?" (trans. Schenke)

In the context of *Philip*, this scene, which has given rise to much speculation about the relationship between Jesus and Mary Magdalene, must be related to Mary's special position as a female disciple. This is neither to be interpreted in a historical perspective nor is an erotic relationship between Jesus and Mary portrayed here. Rather, as with the Beloved Disciple in the Gospel of John, Thomas in the *Gospel of Thomas*, and Judas in the *Gospel of Judas*, Mary is meant to be presented as a female disciple who is especially close to Jesus and who knows about his special role.

Section 99a-b points to the myth that is presupposed, though not expressly narrated: The world came into being through a mistake, for the one who created it wanted to create it imperishable and immortal. He failed and did not achieve what he had hoped, for imperishability does not belong to the world, just as it also does not belong to the one who created the world. Imperishability does not belong to things but to children. In *Philip*, they are the persons who have recognized the truth and are free (110a). This knowledge has been brought by Jesus. It is obtained through union with him. At the same time, this myth contains a criticism of Genesis. The tree of knowledge planted in paradise, which is equated with the law, has mediated only the knowledge of good and evil, but it has not liberated humans from evil and placed them in the sphere of the good. Thus, it brought death to humanity. Here, we are dealing with a noteworthy interpretation of the connection between creation, law, sin (evil), and death, which exhibits echoes of the theology of Paul, and especially of the fifth chapter of Romans. This signals another characteristic feature of *Philip*. The author knows biblical (Old and New Testament) traditions and interprets them within the horizon of a different idea of God, the world, and human beings. This interpretation also finds expression in the passages that deal with the relationship between "Hebrews"—as the Jews are usually called here—and gentiles. Thus, the "Hebrews" do indeed have an advantage over the gentiles or Greeks, but this advantage is not sufficient to attain to salvation. In section 6 it thus says: "When we were Hebrews, we were orphans and had (only) our mother, but when we became Christians, we obtained father and mother" (trans. Schenke). Here, it is interesting that the author reckons himself among those who were themselves "Hebrews" before they were "Christians." Only through this did they obtain a father—i.e., enter into a fully valid relationship to God.

Philip proves to be a writing that interprets the Israelite-Jewish and early Christian traditions on the basis of a myth about the origin of the world and salvation, a myth that clearly differs from the biblical idea of the world and human beings. Jesus, on whose different names—"Christ," "Savior," "Nazarene"—*Philip* reflects (19, 47), has brought humans knowledge about the world and the order of salvation (82, 93b, 107). This is connected especially with his baptism, which is interpreted symbolically as the process of enlightenment (81a, 89, 109). Thus, in the gospel we encounter a distinct form of the reception of Jesus and his coming within the framework of Valentinian teaching about the world, the human being, and salvation.

The *Gospel of Truth*

The so-called *Gospel of Truth* is the third writing in NHC I. The work itself has no title and differs clearly from the previously discussed writings with respect to its literary form. Another version, which is very fragmentarily preserved, appears as the second work in NHC XII. The text is a sermon-like tractate that begins with the words "The gospel of truth is joy for people who have received grace from the Father of truth, that they might know him through the power of the Word" (I 16,31–35; trans. Meyer) It is on this basis, that the designation *Gospel of Truth* was established. Irenaeus, however, also mentions a writing of the Valentinians that they are said to call the *Gospel of Truth* (*Haer.* 3.11.9). Moreover, the Nag Hammadi work shows echoes of Valentinian teaching and has sometimes even been traced back to Valentinus himself as its author. Today, however, an origin from the circle of students of Valentinus is usually assumed, which also corresponds to the information in Irenaeus. Since the teaching of Valentinus was developed further by his students, the *Gospel of the Truth* would need to be regarded as a product of a later stage of Valentinianism. If it were to be identified with the work—or to the Greek Vorlage of the work—to which Irenaeus refers, it would have had to have arisen in the second century. It is more likely, however, that it is a tractate *about* the "gospel of the truth," which could refer either to a specific writing (possibly the one mentioned by Irenaeus) or to the Valentinian teaching as such. In that case, a later date of emergence is also conceivable.

The text can be characterized as a reflection on the knowledge of God the Father, which is mediated through the Savior. The truth of God is contrasted with deception (*planê*), which attempts to prevent Jesus, the teacher of truth, from disclosing the truth to human beings. Jesus is hated by the foolish, who regard themselves as wise—apparently an allusion to the passage on the reversal of wisdom and foolishness in 1 Corinthians (1:18–25)—and, finally, nailed to the cross (I 20,24–35). However, he made known the Father and pointed out the way to him. He called the names of those whom he previously knew (those who are "from above"), led back many out of deception, and removed the deficiency, namely, ignorance about the Father. Therefore, the Son is "the name of the Father." The name itself is invisible, but the Son can be known—an idea that has points of contact with the Gospel of John. By contrast, the person who remains in ignorance is like someone who is tossed about in a restless dream while they sleep (I21,25–23,17). Of the sacraments known from Valentinianism, the anointing is mentioned (I 36,14–37. Those whom the Father has anointed are the ones who have perfected themselves. Their goal is "the place of the blessed," which is also called the "place of rest" (I 42, 37–38).

The *Gospel of Truth* circles around these ideas in a meditative way. In the process, there emerges a quite distinct interpretation of the activity of Jesus, which can be understood—in a certain analogy to the Gospel of John—as a spiritual deepening of the narratives about the activity and teaching of Jesus.

Sources and Studies

Grobel, Kendrick. *The Gospel of Truth: A Valentianian Meditation on the Gospel. Translation from the Coptic and Commentary.* Nashville: Abingdon, 1960.

King, Karen L. "The Place of the *Gospel of Philip* in the Context of Early Christian Claims about Jesus' Marital Status." *NTS* 59 (2013) 565–87.

Meyer, Marvin, ed. *The Nag Hammadi Scriptures: The International Edition.* New York: HarperOne, 2007 ("Gospel of Truth," 36–47).

Schenke, Hans-Martin, trans. "The Gospel of Philip." In *New Testament Apocrypha*, Vol. 1, *Gospels and Related Writings*, edited by Wilhelm Schneemelcher, 179–208. Translated by Robert McL. Wilson. Louisville: Westminster John Knox, 1991.

Smith, Geoffrey S. *Valentinian Christianity: Texts and Translations.* Oakland, CA: University of California Press, 2020.

7

Conclusion

The Significance of the Apocryphal Gospels for the History of Christianity

IN THE FINAL SECTION of this volume some basic aspects shall be summarized to highlight the importance of the apocryphal gospels for studying the formative period of Christianity (and beyond).

The apocryphal gospels present a broad spectrum of interpretations of the person of Jesus. They deal with his birth and childhood, his activity and teaching, his suffering and death, and his appearances and teaching as the Risen One. Some important apocryphal gospels were introduced in this book, but they can be supplemented by many other examples. The composition of texts about Jesus outside the New Testament is restricted neither to antiquity nor to the figures around Jesus that have been discussed in the preceding chapters of this book. Rather, the production of apocryphal (i.e., non-biblical) texts also continued in the Middle Ages, a fact that became clear in the present work especially through the Infancy Gospels and the passion traditions collected in the *Gospel of Nicodemus*. But apocryphal texts were also written later and reach into the present—for example in the form of modern Jesus novels. They encompass a broad field of texts that interpret the person and activity of Jesus from their own perspectives and time and again extract new meaning from his ministry, suffering, death, and resurrection in different epochs of the history of Christianity. Moreover, many of the apocryphal texts have become relevant in later phases of the history of Christianity through translations into different languages and through their use in liturgical contexts. This became clear in the present book through the fact that some of the

CONCLUSION

discussed texts are preserved only in translations, which point to later uses and revisions.

Beyond texts, other forms of the interpretation of the person and activity of Jesus can be identified in different media, such as visual representations (e.g., mosaics, frescoes, and statues), musical compositions, liturgies, films, and buildings. Thus, the numerous representations of his birth and associated episodes (such as the adoration of the magi and the flight to Egypt) as well as visual representations of his suffering on the cross (for example, from the passion piety of the late Middle Ages) present distinct interpretations of the person of Jesus of Nazareth. This already begins in late antiquity, from which visual representations of the birth of Jesus and other episodes from his activity are attested on sarcophagi, frescoes, and mosaics. Likewise, we also find the first representations of his crucifixion. In music, examples include the Christmas and passion music of Heinrich Schütz and Johann Sebastian Bach as well as Felix Mendelssohn Bartholdy's impressive interpretations of the birth and suffering of Jesus. In terms of Jesus films, mention could be made of *Jesus of Montreal* and the musical *Jesus Christ Superstar*, which interpret the activity of Jesus from the perspective of the late twentieth century. A distinct form of the reception of Jesus can be found in rituals and liturgies. In these, a direct encounter between believers and the person of Jesus is established, in which biblical and yet also extra-biblical texts play a role. Finally, buildings and places—for example, caves or tombs—have also become sites of memory of Christianity, which take their orientation from early Christian, biblical and extra-biblical traditions.

In this way, the apocryphal gospels open our eyes to commemorative spaces in which the person of Jesus has been interpreted and appropriated in diverse ways in the history of Christianity. The receptions developed thereby often go beyond the Gospels of the New Testament, supplement the representations of Jesus there, and develop their own forms of interpretation and reception of his activity. Not least, the apocryphal gospels thereby demonstrate that the biblical texts were surrounded from the beginning with interpretations that made them fruitful for different situations and thus contributed to the Bible's ability to be "not a dead letter" but "a life-giving Spirit."

The apocryphal gospels do not form a unity. They were never assembled together in a way that was comparable to the New Testament and did not serve as the basis of a distinct community alongside emerging Christianity. Rather, we are dealing with texts that have very different content and literary character—legends about the child Jesus; narratives about Jesus' activity and suffering that have points of contact with the New Testament Gospels but can also deviate from them or go beyond them; philosophical teachings about the origin of the world, the creation of the human being, and the ascent of the soul into the divine sphere; meditations on the significance of the coming of Jesus into the world and much more. Thus, the apocryphal gospels reveal a much larger spectrum of interpretations than what we find in the Gospels of the New Testament. The designation "gospel" must also be understood in a broader sense. It refers not only to biographical Jesus stories but also to texts that have very different content and literary character, with their commonality consisting in the fact that they convey relevant information about Jesus, his way, and his teaching.

The great diversity of the gospel literature of early Christianity and beyond has led to the question of from where the Christian church should take its orientation in its connection to Jesus. It was exactly this question that led to the distinction of the four "canonical" Gospels from the "apocryphal" gospels. Even though, as a consequence, the "canonical Gospels" obtained a much more prominent status than the "apocryphal" gospels, Christianity's picture of Jesus was never determined solely by the Gospels of the New Testament. The Infancy Gospels, the *Gospel of Nicodemus*, additions to the Gospels of the New Testament, and sayings of Jesus outside the canonical Gospels were part of the Jesus tradition from an early point in time. Through the discovery of long-lost texts since the nineteenth century, the spectrum has been clearly expanded again. This has scarcely changed the historical findings about the activity and fate of Jesus. The apocryphal gospels can allow us, however, to recognize various themes and associations that have been connected with the figure of Jesus in the history of Christianity. In this way, they expand the biblical picture of Jesus and challenge it through competing representations. The apocryphal gospels are, therefore, an indispensable element of a contemporary engagement with the impact of Jesus of Nazareth.

The apocryphal gospels have different tradition and reception histories. Some of them were known from a very early time—at least in certain spheres of tradition—and have correspondingly influenced the perception of the person of Jesus in Christian piety. Others, such as the texts that became known through the findings at Nag Hammadi, were long known only by name or not at all, and only surfaced again more recently through the discovery of manuscripts. These discoveries—to which new ones could again be added, as shown by the recently discovered *Unknown Berlin Gospel* and the *Gospel of Judas*—place the history of early Christianity in a more comprehensive light. They make clear that the teaching of Jesus could be connected to philosophical themes such as the origin and goal of the human being, knowledge of the self and the world, and liberation from earthly ties as a way to true humanity. They show that the activity of Jesus could be embedded in more comprehensive presentations of the world and the human being, which sometimes included a polemical reinterpretation of the origin of the world and humans, as recounted in the first chapters of Genesis. Here, they often advocate the view that the historical situation of the life of Jesus is overcome by the much more far-reaching teaching of the Risen One and disclosed for new contexts. Others, in turn, emphasize the Jewish context of Jesus and the Jewish traditions that surround his activity and point thereby to the enduring significance of these traditions in early Christianity. In this way, a variety of receptions and reworkings of the activity and fate of Jesus come into view, in which a broad spectrum of social and religious formations is simultaneously reflected. Thus, through the apocryphal texts, the history of early Christianity becomes more multifaceted in theological, philosophical, religious, and social respects.

The apocryphal gospels are not "hidden" texts, though this could be suggested by the designation "apocryphal." Some of them do, in fact, designate themselves as "apocryphal" (i.e., "hidden") and seek to mediate a higher teaching that is accessible only to the initiated. Others, however, understand themselves as vivid texts that make the person of Jesus meaningful for their own time. All of these texts, however, are readily accessible through textual editions and translations and are by no means "secret." Even the texts that designate themselves as "apocryphal" seek, of course, to be read, which is why their self-designation as "apocryphal" is probably best understood in the sense of their self-characterization as texts that mediate especially important insights. For Christianity, these texts played an important role for the interpretation of the activity and fate of Jesus from the beginning. Their rediscovery and the intense engagement with them in more recent times contributes to a clearer understanding of the interpretive and commemorative spaces that surround the person of Jesus in the history of Christianity.

Subject Index

Ananias, 70
Archons, 65, 87–89, 92, 101
Athanasius, 8

Basilides, 5–6

Cerinthus, 78
Chromatius, 26
Clement of Alexandria, xi, 4, 6, 16, 36, 38, 41–44, 96
Codex Berolinensis Gnosticus, 80–82, 85
Codex Bobiensis, 77
Codex Cantabrigiensis, 53–54
Codex Sabaiticus, 23
Codex Sinaiticus, 76
Codex Tchacos, 62, 73, 80
Codex Vaticanus, 76

Didymus the Blind, xi, 37, 54, 67
Diogenes Laertius, 95
Docetism / docetic, 5, 29, 57, 79

Epicurus, 95
Epiphanius of Salamis, xi, 40–42, 64, 71, 100
Eusebius, 4, 5, 13, 35, 38, 54, 56–57, 71, 77

Flavius Josephus, 47

Gnosticism / gnostic, 10, 42, 50, 62–65, 73, 79, 83, 85–86, 89, 92, 96, 98, 100
God-bearer, 17, 22
Golden Legend (*Legenda aurea*), 73

Gregory of Nazianzus, 49
Gregory of Nyssa, 77

Heliodorus, 26
Hippolytus, xi, 41–42, 50
Historical Jesus scholarship, ix–x, 7, 11–12, 14–15, 32, 49, 60, 73, 93–95, 102, 108–109

Irenaeus of Lyon, xi, 1, 2, 3, 4, 6, 23, 40, 50, 62–64, 85–86, 89, 100, 104

Jerome, xi, 17, 26–27, 36–39, 41, 77
Justin Martyr, xii, 3, 16, 71, 90

Nag Hammadi, xii, 13, 22, 24, 62–63, 65, 80, 82, 85, 93, 98–99, 103, 105, 108
Nag Hammadi Codices
  Codex I, 89, 98, 104
  Codex II, 24, 85, 93, 98–99
  Codex III, 65, 82, 85, 92, 98
  Codex IV, 85, 98
  Codex V, 62
  Codex VII, 62
  Codex XII, 104
nomina sacra, 44–45, 48
Nussberger-Tchacos, Frieda, 62

Origen, xii, 5–6, 13, 16, 21, 36–37, 40–42, 67
Oxyrhynchus, 31, 48, 50–52, 55, 58–59, 73–74, 80, 82, 86, 93, 98

Papias of Hierapolis, 35, 54

SUBJECT INDEX

Papyrus Bodmer V, 17–19
Plato / Platonic, 36, 82, 89, 94

Rule of Benedict, 27

Serapion, 4, 31–32, 56–58

Tatian, 26
Tertullian, xii, 13, 16, 71

Valentinus / Valentinianism, 2, 6, 100, 102, 104–5

Author Index

Aasgaard, Reidar, 23, 32

Bell, H. Idris, 44, 55
Beyers, Rita, 32
Bickell, G., 69
Bockmuehl, Markus, 12
Boer, Esther de, 98
Bouriant, Urbain, 57, 73
Bovon, François, 12
Budge, Ernest Alfred Wallis, 26
Burke, Tony, ii, x, 23–24, 32, 55

Cartlidge, David R., 12
Čeplö, Slavomír, 30–32
Clivas, Claire, 32
Coles, R. Alan, 58, 73

DeConick, April D., 98

Ehrman, Bart D., x, 4, 18, 53–55, 73
Elliott, J. K., 12, 55
Emmel, Stephen, 68, 73

Fabricius, Johann Albert, 8, 10, 12, 17
Foster, Paul, 12, 73

Gathercole, Simon, 73, 98
Geoltrain, Pierre, 12
Gijsel, Jan, 27, 32
Grenfell, Bernard P., 31–32, 48, 51, 55, 93, 98
Grobel, Kendrick, 105

Hartenstein, Judith, 98
Hawk, Brandon W., 27, 29, 32
Hedrick, Charles W., 66, 73

Hills, Julian V., ii, 98
Hock, Ronald, 18, 32
Holmes, Michael, 12, 43, 59
Hunt, Arthur S., 31–32, 48, 51, 55, 93, 98

Jacobi, Christine, 13
James, Montague Rhodes, 28–29, 32

Kaestli, Jean-Daniel, 12, 28, 32
Kasser, Rodolphe, 61, 73
King, Karen L., 98, 105
Klauck, Hans-Joseph, 12
Kraus, Thomas J., 55, 74
Kruger, Michael J., 55

Ladenheim, Alex, 18, 33
Landau, Brent, ii, x, 12, 32, 55
Layton, Bentley, 74, 98
Lessing, Gotthold Ephraim, 11–12
Lienhard, J.T., 6, 13
Lührmann, Dieter, 13, 55, 59, 69

Markschies, Christoph, 13
McNamara, Martin, 32
Merton, Wilfred, 50, 55
Meyer, Marvin, 83–84, 92, 98, 104–5
Mingana, Alphonse, 30, 33
Mirecki, Paul A., 66, 73

Nicklas, Tobias, 55, 74

Otero, Aurelio de Santos, 13

Petersen, Silke, 98
Pleše, Zlatko, x, 4, 12, 53–54

AUTHOR INDEX

Plisch, Uwe-Karsten, 66, 74, 79
Porter, Stanley E., 55
Postel, Guillaume, 17, 33
Provera, Mario E., 25–26, 33

Rees, Brinley R., 50

Schenke, Hans-Martin, 66, 73–74, 101–3, 105
Schmidt, Carl, 68, 74
Schneemelcher, Wilhelm, 13
Schneider, Gerhard, 18, 33
Schröter, Jens, 13
Shoemaker, Stephen J., 98
Sike, Heinrich, 25–26, 33
Skeat, Theodore C., 44, 55
Smith, Geoffrey S., 105
Spittler, Janet, x
Strycker, Émile de, 18, 33

Suciu, Alin, 66–68, 74

Terian, Abraham, 33
Thilo, Johannes Carolus, 13, 27
Tischendorf, Constantin von, 13, 18, 23–24, 26–27, 70
Tuckett, Christopher, 98

Vuong, Lily, 18, 33

Waldstein, Michael, 86–87, 98
Watson, Francis, 13, 98
Wayment, Thomas A., 13, 18, 33
Williams, Francis E., 88–89, 91, 98
Williamson, Geoffrey A., 5
Wisse, Frederik, 86–87, 98
Wurst, Gregor, 62, 73

Zelyck, Lorne, 46, 55

www.ingramcontent.com/pod-product-compliance
Lightning Source LLC
Chambersburg PA
CBHW030903170426
43193CB00009BA/728